CULT PERFUMES

Tessa Williams

CULT PERFUMES
The World's Most Exclusive Perfumeries

Tessa Williams

2021

MERRELL
LONDON · NEW YORK

7 Introduction

CULT PERFUMES

19 Amouage

25 Angela Flanders

29 Annick Goutal

33 Antonia's Flowers

39 L'Artisan Parfumeur

45 Carthusia

53 Clive Christian

59 Creed

67 Diptyque

73 Floris

79 Frédéric Malle

85 Grossmith

93 Houbigant

97 Jo Malone London

101 Krigler

107 Lorenzo Villoresi

113 Lubin

121 Maison Francis Kurkdjian

127 Miller Harris

133 Nicolaï

139 Ormonde Jayne

145 Penhaligon's

151 Robert Piguet

157 Roja Dove

163 Santa Maria Novella

169 Serge Lutens

174 Niche Brands

FEATURES

43 Olivia Giacobetti

57 Rose de Mai

83 Edmond Roudnitska

99 Jo Loves

131 Jean Carles

155 Fracas

182 Glossary

185 Further Reading

186 Museums and Collections

188 Picture credits

189 Index

Introduction

Imagine a world without perfume; how sterile, lifeless and devoid of emotion it would be. Scent can be uplifting and transporting. Wearing it is rather like being followed around by your own orchestra, or having an interior designer to create a beautiful space for you, throwing bouquets of roses in your wake. Perfume has its own energy – its own noise, almost. You can be assured that your spirits will lift as soon as you put it on, whether it is your signature scent or part of your wardrobe of fragrances. 'To emit a scent is the farthest an objective reality is able to go towards dematerializing and becoming pure idea', says Jean-Claude Ellena, one of the leading 'noses' (perfumers) of the twentieth century and head perfumer at Hermès. Perfume is still one of the finest presents anyone can bestow. Two of the gifts brought to Jesus Christ as a baby – myrrh and frankincense – were perfumes.

In choosing a perfume you will go on a journey, through fields of patchouli, jasmine and tuberose, and through the feelings and emotions bottled so carefully by artist perfumers. Scent itself goes everywhere. It can wind its way through doors, windows and walls; it crosses boundaries. Scent is ageless and raceless, and, as the perfumer Roja Dove says, 'Perfume can make the lady of eighty feel as though she is eighteen again.' It can transform the mediocre moment into something ravishing and magical.

One of the qualities of perfume is its fleeting life, its short-lived beauty. A great deal of time and effort goes into making a few drops of liquid that will evaporate into thin air. It is not like the painter's canvas, which can be looked at over the centuries, or a musical score, which can be replayed and reinterpreted again and again. Evidence of the vast collection of a perfumista survives only in the glass bottles remaining on the dressing table.

Perfume goes back as far as human history itself. One of the earliest recorded perfume recipes is in the book of Exodus, when Moses was instructed by God to make an oil of myrrh, cinnamon, calamus (sweet flag), cassia (Chinese cinnamon) and olive oil to anoint the Ark of the Covenant (30:22–25).

The first perfumers were ancient Egyptian priests, who blended flowers

Opposite: *Rosa* 'Fantin-Latour', a beautiful, classic rose, has a sweet, warm, intoxicating fragrance evident in many perfumes.

Above: An ancient Egyptian tablet in the Louvre, Paris, depicts a woman dousing herself with perfume. Cleopatra was known to dab civet on her eyebrows before meeting Mark Antony, to increase his passion.

Right: A first-century fresco from the Villa Farnesina in Rome shows a woman pouring perfume into a flask.

Far right: A miniature from Avicenna's *Canon of Medicine* in the University Library of Bologna shows a scene at a pharmacy.

Below: An English sixteenth-century silver-gilt pomander with four open compartments used to hold perfumes.

and juices into offerings for their gods in workshops attached to their temples. They even imagined that perfume represented the sweat of the gods. As they prayed, they held incense burners to send the smoke towards the sky, where they believed the scent would be inhaled by the gods. They used several different resins, including that from the turpentine tree; in about 2000 BC this was replaced by frankincense and myrrh. The Egyptians also used perfume for embalming the dead, as they believed in the transmigration of the soul, and incense was burned for its mind-altering and sedative qualities.

The Romans, ever lovers of luxury, were enthusiastic users of perfume; indeed, the word 'perfume' itself is from the Latin *per fumum*, 'through smoke'. So enamoured were they by the smell of good things that they scented the doves that flew around at their feasts, incorporated perfume in the walls of their buildings and slept on mattresses stuffed with roses.

After the fall of the Roman empire, the culture and benefits of perfume were lost to the West for nearly a thousand years, although it continued to be used widely in Islamic cultures. Mosques were built using mortar mixed with musk, so that scent would emanate from the building when the sun shone on it. Avicenna, the eleventh-century Arabian alchemist and physician, is reputed to be the first perfumer of the modern age. He stumbled on the recipe for rose water while attempting to extract the 'soul' of the holy rose of Islam.

In the Middle Ages, crusaders returning from the Middle East brought back to the West scents and spices that had long been forgotten. Venice, where sea merchants unloaded their cargoes of spices, musk and silks, became a centre for the trade in perfume, ranking in Europe with Florence, Paris and later London.

It was Catherine de' Medici who put Paris firmly on the perfume map, when she went to France in 1533 to marry Henry II. She travelled with her own perfumer, René de Florentin, and is credited with having introduced a new level of style to France. Florentin set up a shop on a Paris bridge, the Pont au Change, and Catherine had many other perfumers vie for her attention. Her influence was not restricted to fragrance,

however: she also brought with her to France high-heeled shoes, corsets, ballet, Italian cooking and the habit of eating with a fork. In the year of her marriage, the monks of Officina Profumo Farmaceutica di Santa Maria Novella in Florence created Acqua della Regina for her, and it is still sold today.

Another queen of France, Marie Antoinette (1755–1793), was said to be fanatical about perfume, and spent a fortune on it. She, too, had her own perfumer, Jean-Louis Fargeon. She adored the fragrances of Houbigant, and is reputed to have worn its scents on her way to the gallows. In 2005 the Parisian company was resurrected, and in 2009 its century-old classic scent Quelques Fleurs was remade.

Marie Antoinette's spirit lives on: in 2006, more than 200 years after her death, the star perfumer Francis Kurkdjian re-created her signature scent with the writer Elisabeth de Feydeau. Called M.A. Sillage de la Reine, the new fragrance was built with the original ingredients – rose, iris, orange blossom, tuberose and jasmine – and updated with two fresh notes, grey amber and tonkin musk.

Both Catherine de' Medici and Marie Antoinette were keen wearers of leather gloves, which – being cured with urine – needed to be specially soaked in perfume to mask their strong smell. French aristocrats also wore them so that they could hold a finger to their nose to shield themselves from the smells surrounding them. The fashion for these gloves sowed the seeds of the perfume industry.

In the late eighteenth century the town of Grasse in the south-west of France,

Top: Marie Antoinette (1755–1793), shown in an Austrian portrait of *c.* 1767 (in the Schoenbrunn Palace, Vienna), was one of perfume's earliest and most devoted aficionados.

Above: Portrait of Catherine de' Medici, another great lover of perfume, by Santi di Tito (sixteenth century; in the Uffizi Gallery, Florence).

Above, clockwise from top left: Lavender grows in the warm climate of Provence; jasmine flowers are picked in the Domaine de Manon, Grasse; tuberose for perfume is weighed in Mysore, India; jasmine flowers during the cold-extraction procedure in a perfume factory in Grasse.

already known for its scented gloves and other leather products, became the world's leading centre for the manufacture of perfume. Its warm climate proved to be perfect for growing the flowers needed for perfume, and the town still produces more than two-thirds of France's natural aromas, including the special Rose de Mai (see p. 57). The town produces more than 27 tons of jasmine annually, and houses the perfume factories of Fragonard, Galimard, Molinard and Robertet; Fragonard has had its own museum there since 1921. Many perfumers study, and eventually work, there. Lyn Harris of Miller Harris, for example, spent her final years of study in Grasse, and it was there that she gained the knowledge and impetus to start her own company in London in 2000.

The second oldest perfumery still in existence today, after Santa Maria Novella, is Floris, which was established in 1730 by Juan Famenias Floris at 89 Jermyn Street, London. Nearly 300 years later it occupies the same shop and is owned by the same family.

Towards the end of the eighteenth century the perfume industry began to take hold, with the classic house of Creed beginning in 1760, that of Houbigant in 1775 and that of Lubin in 1798. As the industry expanded, so did the ways in which fragrances were created. Modern perfumery was born with the discovery by scientists of synthetic formulations of natural scents, and between 1850 and 1921 the production of perfume changed more than it had done in the previous 4000 years. One important synthetic ingredient, coumarin (created in 1868), resembled the smell of hay. It was derived from the tonka bean, and could be made at a fraction of the price of the real thing. In 1882 the perfumer Paul Parquet used coumarin to make Houbigant's fragrance Fougère Royale, the scent that would change the nature of modern perfumery.

The discovery of synthetics brought about the birth of such exciting fragrances as Jicky (1889), L'Heure Bleue (1912) and Mitsouko (1919), all by Guerlain. Jicky involved the clever combination of three different scent molecules, while Fougère Royale made use of only one. Other key fragrances of the time were L.T. Piver's Le Trèfle Incarnat (1898) and Guerlain's Après L'Ondée (1906), both of which made great use of anisic aldehyde.

The entrée of one of perfume's all-time classics, Chanel No. 5, was made possible by the scientific advances of the previous few decades. It was created in Cannes in 1921 by the Russian perfumer Ernest Beaux, who came up with the scent that Gabrielle Chanel sought in her quest to define herself as a designer of modernity. She described it as 'a bouquet of abstract flowers'. Chanel was obsessed with the number five, and launched the new perfume on the fifth day of the fifth month that year. She used it to scent her shop's dressing rooms, and gave bottles as presents to a select few of her high-society friends. The success of the fragrance was immediate and phenomenal, and 10 million bottles are still sold every year. Marilyn Monroe, when asked what she wore to bed, answered, 'Just a few drops of No. 5', and the scent's iconic status was

cemented when a bottle was added to the permanent collection of the Museum of Modern Art in New York in 1959. It also became the subject of a screen print by the artist Andy Warhol, reproduced by Chanel on a limited-edition box in 1982.

Gabrielle Chanel also began in earnest the trend for fashion designers to have their own fragrances, although the couturier Paul Poiret had preceded her by a decade with Parfums de Rosine (1911), named after his daughter. Other fashion designers – including Jeanne Lanvin, Jeanne Paquin, Lucien Lelong and Madeleine Vionnet – followed suit, all keen to have perfumes that complemented their clothes. This cemented what is now a lucrative relationship between designer and perfumer.

Few people have been more influential in the history and development of perfume than François Coty, one of the great pioneers. Born Joseph Marie François Spoturno in Corsica in 1874, and descended from an aunt of Napoléon Bonaparte, he moved to France at an early age. He changed his name to the more French-sounding Coty (after his mother's maiden name, the Corsican Coti) when he married. He began working in Grasse in his twenties and later set up his own perfume laboratory in his apartment in Paris, with a loan from his grandmother. He created his first perfume, La Rose Jacqueminot, in 1904. At first he sold his fragrances in plain apothecary-style bottles, to be decanted at home into something more decorative, but he quickly realized that he could charge more for his perfumes if they were packaged in ornate

Frankincense is one of the earliest recorded perfume ingredients. The fragrance is obtained from the resin of trees in the genus *Boswellia*.

Estée Lauder, Youth Dew, 1953

Giorgio Beverly Hills, Giorgio, 1981

bottles. In 1908 he worked with the glass-maker René Lalique to produce the beautiful glass bottles that would make him very wealthy. He was also the first to understand the value of marketing, and to realize that offering perfumes at various strengths and in various sizes of bottle, at different prices, would appeal to a wider range of customers.

Coty developed many landmark fragrances in his time, including L'Origan (1905), Ambre Antique (1910), Chypre (1917) and L'Aimant of 1927 (an aldehyde-rich perfume, Coty's answer to Chanel No. 5). He also amassed great riches, had many love affairs, bought and sold chateaux and became a newspaper magnate (he owned *Le Figaro* for some years, and in 1928 started another newspaper, *L'Ami du peuple*, which became a klaxon for his extremely right-wing views). He became more tyrannical as he grew older, and died alone of pneumonia in 1934. His wife, aghast at his indiscretions, had divorced him years before. She sold Coty to the American drug company Pfizer in 1963; in 1992 the brand was bought by Benckiser Consumer Products, the United States arm of the family-owned German household-products company Johannes A. Benckiser. Coty is now one of the largest cosmetics and fragrance companies in the world, and produces most of the celebrity fragrances, including the multimillion-selling perfumes of Jennifer Lopez, Lady Gaga, David Beckham and Beyoncé Knowles. François Coty's name also lives on in the annual François Coty Perfumer Award, a great honour bestowed on up-and-coming independent perfumers.

Through Coty's example of clever marketing and scientific developments throughout the world, perfume-making started to become a huge industry, and in the 1940s and 1950s more robust perfumes were created. The landmark fragrance Miss Dior was launched in 1947 by Dior. It was created by Jean Carles (see p. 131), one of the world's most talented perfumers, who later became anosmic and could not smell anything he created. Balmain's Vent Vert was also launched in 1947. Robert Piguet's Fracas (1948), made by Germaine Cellier, still makes waves when it is worn today (see p. 155). Although the formula was tweaked when the scent was re-created by the perfumer Aurelien Guichard and reissued in 1998, it is still reminiscent of the original.

The year 1950 saw the launch of Piguet's Baghari. Three years later Estée Lauder's Youth Dew was introduced; it sold 50,000 bottles in its first year, and by 1984 more than 150,000,000 bottles had been sold, securing it a place among the highest-selling perfumes of all time. Other perfumes from the 1950s are Caron's Muguet du Bonheur (1952), Premier Muguet by Bourjois (1955) and Diorissimo by Dior (created by Edmond Roudnitska in 1956). Diorissimo stood out among lily-of-the-valley perfumes for its striking faithfulness to the scent of the flower. Unlike that of other flowers, the smell of lily of the valley cannot be extracted, and Roudnitska's achievement using synthetic ingredients made history and revolutionized his standing as a perfumer.

Roudnitska (1905–1996; see p. 83) was perhaps one of the most uniquely talented perfumers to emerge from France. He was born in Nice and began his career in Grasse at the age of twenty-one, with no formal training and no family connections. In 1946 he started his own company, Arts et Parfums – a private laboratory for the creation of fragrances – near Grasse. 'The more we understand odours, the more they end up possessing us. They live within us, becoming an integral part of us, participating in a new function within us', he said in his book *Une Vie au Service du Parfum* (*A Life in the Service of Perfume*; 1991).

Roudnitska's talent for creating scents using completely new materials knew no bounds. As well as Diorissimo, he created Rochas Femme (1944) and Eau d'Hermès (1951), going on to compose the groundbreaking Eau Sauvage for Dior in 1966. His range and depth of work were recognized posthumously by the cult perfumer Frédéric Malle, who included Roudnitska's scent Le Parfum de Thérèse in his Editions de Parfums range in 2000.

In the 1960s and 1970s new spicy and oriental perfumes came on the scene. Calèche (1961) was made for Hermès by the French nose Guy Robert, who went on to create perfume for the independent label Amouage in 1983. Rive Gauche (1971), created by the perfumer Michael Hy for Yves Saint Laurent, came out in a blue, black and silver bottle to commemorate the moon landing of 1969. Then in 1977 Yves Saint Laurent launched Opium, causing great shock and anguish with its drugs connotations.

In the 1970s jewellers also began producing scents. Van Cleef & Arpels introduced First in 1976, and Must de Cartier was launched in 1981. In the late 1980s the high-end jeweller Joel Arthur Rosenthal (also known as JAR) established his own hyper-exclusive perfume shop on Place Vendôme in Paris, opposite the Ritz. The store has no display window; it does not advertise and it opens its doors only to a select few, including Gwyneth Paltrow, Elle Macpherson, the socialite Marella Agnelli and Princess Firyal of Jordan.

It was perhaps during the 1980s, when perfumes were becoming ever larger and stronger – rather like the shoulder pads of the time – that niche perfumes began to establish themselves in reaction. Giorgio by Giorgio Beverly Hills (1981), Calvin Klein's Obsession (1985) and Dior's Poison (1985) were so powerful that they could be smelled before the wearer arrived. Some restaurants in New York and Los Angeles banned the wearing of Giorgio, as its tuberose scent was so potent. Fragrances were being launched worldwide simultaneously, and the perfume industry had become obsessed with marketing. Seeking immediate success, the mass-market companies wanted everyone to wear the same fragrance.

When the former model and classical pianist Annick Goutal launched her soft and delicate Eau d'Hadrien, a unisex scent, in 1981, a new standard was set. Subtle, understated artisan perfumes began to take hold. Such brands have little or no advertising budget, and so everything is focused on the product, which tends to speak for itself. L'Artisan Parfumeur had

François Coty was the founder of the Coty empire and the father of modern perfumery. He created such everlasting classics as Chypre (1917) and L'Aimant (1927).

anticipated the trend five years earlier, and began to commission key perfumers to create their own fragrances.

At the beginning of the twenty-first century the world of niche fragrances was being set alight by the establishment of many independent perfume houses. Ormonde Jayne, Miller Harris, Jo Malone and Antonia's Flowers are all one-woman companies that have gained international cult status. There also began the resurgence of former classic perfume houses, such as the Crown Perfumer, founded in 1872 and brought back to life by the interior designer Clive Christian in 1999. Christian went on to produce his own cult perfume with No. 1 (2001), the 'World's Most Expensive' perfume. Simon and Amanda Brooke re-established the Victorian perfumery Grossmith in 2009 because of a family connection, and remade many of the perfumes that Queen Victoria had known and loved.

The undisputed king of the cult trend, however, is the indomitable Frédéric Malle (born 1962). With his Editions de Parfums range, he commissions emerging and established perfumers and put their names on the bottles, thus making them stars. He has created an appreciation of the artists of the perfume industry, the noses and perfume-makers themselves, and has set the bar for all cult perfumers. 'Although perfumers, like most artists, are inspired each day by colours, music or any other elements that they encounter in their lives, our business – like abstract painting and music – is anything but

intellectual. Perfumery is a sensual art par excellence. At the beginning of the development of a fragrance, perfumery calls on the right side of our brain', he explains in his book *On Perfume Making* (2011)

Of all the human senses, smell is the strongest trigger of emotion, and perfume can do many things. Who is not moved by the sudden hint of a fragrance that sets off a spiral of reminiscence? For the writer Marcel Proust, each hour of our life as it passes is stored away in a scent, a taste or a sensation that, if found again, can trigger a memory. His most famous work, *A la recherche du temps perdu (In Search of Lost Time, 1913–27)*, was built on this belief. Smells can remind us of our first love, of romances, friendships and family, and even of pets or cars (one perfumer has been asked to replicate the smell of a car exhaust; see Union, p. 181).

Perfume has also historically been used to cure illness. As early as 1381, the rose water and orange water made by the monks of Santa Maria Novella were used as an antiseptic to clean houses of bubonic plague. In the seventeenth and eighteenth centuries doctors promoted the use of perfume to combat infection. Perfumes were also used as remedies for many physical or mental disorders, including hysteria, amenorrhoea, depression, hypochondria, headaches and even the common cold. It was discovered in the nineteenth century that cinnamon and thyme could kill the bacteria that causes typhoid fever in less than an hour; lavender had the same effect, although it took longer (about twelve hours).

Above: The saleroom of the Santa Maria Novella perfumery in Florence sells fragrances created since the fourteenth century in a magnificent setting.

Right: A sixteenth-century perfume-oil vase is part of Santa Maria Novella's collection.

Perfumes were dispensed by apothecaries alongside medical remedies, and many are still stocked by pharmacies. Several monasteries had laboratories where the monks made perfume; Carthusia, where the monks' own recipes were originally used, is one on the island of Capri. Santa Maria Novella, which originated in the thirteenth century, still has its heart in a former monastery building in Florence. The perfumery has now spread its wings all over the world, with stores as far afield as Korea, China, Japan and South Africa showing its great cult appeal.

One of the earliest modern perfumes had great beautifying qualities. Legend has it that in the late fourteenth century a fragrance was created for a queen of Hungary. Legend has it that this Hungary Water, a cologne of rosemary, made her so beautiful that she married the king of Poland at the tender age of seventy-five. The independent British perfumer Angela Flanders created her own version of Hungary Water in 2003 in homage to this great scent.

Few perfumes date in the way that clothes do, and one can wear a perfume from the 1920s (Chanel No. 5, Guerlain's Shalimar) as easily as one can dab on a scent created in the 2010s. It is hard to imagine putting on a shirt or a pair of shoes created in 1920 and still feeling ravishing today.

Many perfume ingredients have not changed over the years, and the palette of the perfumer is to be found in various countries. The strongly, almost carnally scented tuberose grows in Italy, Morocco and India; lavender, orange blossom, lemon and bergamot come from Sicily and Calabria in southern Italy; and iris root from Italy. The jasmine that grows in such profusion in Grasse has a heady, sensual scent, and when the small, white, star-shaped flowers with their red hearts are picked they make a little squeaking noise – said to be the flower complaining. Their fragrance is so delicate that 1 tonne of petals (8 million flowers) is needed to make just 2.5 kg of concrete essence, which in turn will yield just over 1 kg of the fabulous absolute.

Flowers and roots provide a soft, gentle note, but it is the animal ingredients that are responsible for the power and depth of perfume, and which also work as a fixative, helping the perfume to stay on the skin for longer. Musk comes from the musk deer and ambergris from the sperm whale. Civet was the first animal fixative to be used, and some Victorian men wore it on its own, to cover up their own smell. Castoreum, a substance with a strong leathery smell, comes from the beavers of Canada and Russia. Legislation now restricts the use of animal products, and most perfumers use synthetic animal notes.

The ingredients may have been largely the same for centuries, but the way in which perfumes are made and extracted has changed in many ways over the years. One of the oldest methods – first used by the Egyptians – is enfleurage, whereby glass plates held in a wooden frame are covered in a thin layer of watered-down fat and flowers, leaving a scented fatty residue. It is labour-intensive, as the

An advertisement for Mitsouko (1919) by Guerlain in an English magazine in 1938 dares to ask, 'Are you her type?'

flowers have to be removed from the fat by hand afterwards. Enfleurage was the process so sensually described by Patrick Süskind in his novel *Perfume: The Story of a Murderer* (1985):

The souls of these noblest of blossoms [jasmine and tuberose] could not be simply ripped from them, they had to be methodically coaxed away. In a special impregnating room, the flowers were strewn on glass plates smeared with cool oil or wrapped in oil-soaked cloths; there they would die in their sleep. It took three or four days for them to wither and exhale their scent into the adhering oil. Then they were carefully plucked off and new blossoms spread out. This procedure was repeated a good ten, twenty times, and it was September before the pomade had drunk its fill and the fragrant oil could be pressed from the cloths.

Almost as old as enfleurage is distillation, where odorous molecules are evaporated from the raw materials with steam, lowering the temperature at which evaporation occurs and thus decreasing the risk of damage to the delicate organic material. Until the Middle Ages, perfumers could use only the water distilled from such flowers and plants as roses or orange blossom. In 1880 a new method, volatile solvent extraction, was discovered, where the steam used in distillation is replaced by alcohol, and it became possible to extract the aroma from plants that have only a very faint scent. After putting the plants through various processes, a material known as a 'concrete' is obtained. Citrus expression is a simpler form of extracting the oils from the peel of citrus fruit. With the advent in the 1980s of 'headspace technology', whereby molecules of scent in the air around an object are analysed to 'extract' the fragrance of that object, the opportunity arose for the perfumer to create more unusual aromas. In just a century, the perfumer's palette has increased by more than 2000 notes.

Right: Perfumery processes: Enfleurage (right) at the Fragonard factory, Grasse; filling a perfume still (far right).

Opposite, top: An enormous image of a bottle of Chanel No. 5 envelops the Musée d'Orsay, Paris, January 2011.

Opposite, bottom: The iconic Chanel No. 5, created by Ernest Beaux in 1921, remains one of the highest-selling perfumes of all time.

Many perfumers still work with a perfume organ, a fan-shaped wooden object reminiscent of the musical instrument after which it is named. The small bottles of oils and extracts are arranged in rows for the perfumer to draw from for composition, in the manner of notes on a keyboard.

The market is always growing. Celebrities vie to enrich the worth of their brands with more and more new perfumes, even though there are already more than 300,000 designer scents. As the niche perfumes grow and more people become interested in them, one notices why so many people are turning their back on the huge conglomerates. The well-known perfume on display in every duty-free shop from Dubai to Hong Kong to New York is not the one everyone wants to wear. The selective customer will search out the small artisan perfumer, quietly working away at his craft and producing scents for love, rather than to a marketer's brief. Gone are the days when everyone wanted to wear the same scent, and the opportunities to smell unique are now limitless. Perfume reflects our society, and there will always be something more special and lasting – for those who appreciate the artist's way, the hand-blown glass bottles and the specially sourced materials – than the ubiquitous blockbuster fragrances. Even in times of recession, a small luxury like a bottle of a cult perfume can go a long way. People are more willing to spend money on such a unique possession than on a whole designer suit, for example.

The number of emerging young niche perfumers is further evidence of

this growing trend. One of these is the Icelandic artist Andrea Maack (see p. 174), who turned to perfume from the visual arts as an extra means of expression and because she could see there was something exciting happening of which she wanted to be part.

When the *New York Times* appointed a perfume critic, Chandler Burr, in 2006, it recognized that perfume was an art form. Burr wrote, 'The creation of fragrance is one of the highest art forms ... the equivalent of painting for sight and music for hearing, and this column is about treating perfume as the art that it is.' The art of perfume does indeed involve a love and appreciation of something higher than mere scent in a bottle.

Amouage

Perfumes are more than just beautiful scents. They are a philosophy, a representation of life, living, who we are and how we want to define ourselves

Christopher Chong

L ike a refreshing spritz of fine fragrance in the midst of a desert, Amouage has become one of the leading perfume houses of the Middle East, gaining a glowing reputation among perfume collectors from all corners of the world. A bespoke brand with a discerning following, it numbers Kate Moss, Pierce Brosnan and George Clooney among its select clientele.

Amouage (pronounced 'amwaj') – a combination of the Arabic for 'waves' and *amour*, the French for 'love' – was established in 1983 in Oman by Sayyid Hamad bin Hamoud al Busaidi, the cousin of the Sultan of Brunei, largely with the aim of restoring the perfume traditions of the Eastern world. Today, the company is run by the founder's son, Sayyid Khalid bin Hamad al Busaidi, and Amouage fragrances are traditionally offered by the Sultan and other members of the Omani royal family to heads of state during official international visits.

Guy Robert, perhaps the most highly regarded perfumer of the time, was engaged to make the first perfume, called simply Gold (1983). Among other fragrances, Robert had created the original Madame Rochas (1960) for Rochas, Calèche (1961), the chypre-and-citrus perfume for Hermès, and Dioressence (1969) for Christian Dior. Robert cites the creation of Gold as the high point of his career. Allowing him to make something so exquisite, with money no object, put Amouage immediately on the perfume map of the world. And by using many key products of the region, most notably silver frankincense, an extremely valuable ingredient, and the rare rock rose, Amouage created a style all its own – as well as one of the most expensive perfumes available to purchase at that time.

Not only did the company spare no expense in the creation of its perfumes, but also it housed them in fabulously ornate bottles, designed by Asprey of London and

Christopher Chong

Opposite: Jubilation 25 Woman was created in 2008 by Christopher Chong and Lucas Sieuzak to commemorate Amouage's twenty-fifth anniversary. It has notes of tarragon, rose and lemon with a base of amber, myrrh and patchouli.

Left: Many of Amouage's products are luxuriously presented. This gold-plated solid perfume compact for travelling is available in several different scents.

made of sterling silver and pure gold. The lid of the men's scent bottle was designed to replicate the ceremonial dagger worn by Omani men, while that of the women's perfume bottle was modelled on the dome of the Sultan Qaboos Grand Mosque, Oman.

In 2006 Amouage went through a core reshuffle, and a new director, David Crickmore, who had previously worked for Alfred Dunhill and other luxury-goods companies, was appointed. Crickmore's aim was to make Amouage an international brand. 'Oman only happens to be the birthplace of Amouage, which doesn't mean that it is an Arabic brand. ... Amouage's mission is to travel and establish itself all over the world', he said at the time. Amouage opened its own store in Muscat in 2008; there is also one in Belgravia, London, and one in Kuala Lumpur, Malaysia, and more will follow around the world.

The Amouage store in London, opened in June 2010, is the brand's third flagship store and one of few boutiques outside the Persian Gulf. The opulent interior befits the luxurious style of the fragrances.

Crickmore appointed a new creative director, Christopher Chong. Born in Hong Kong and raised in New York, Chong had an eclectic artistic background: he ran his own modelling agency to fund his degree before studying for an MA at the University of London. After working in business development and as a journalist, he trained as an opera singer before being approached by Crickmore. Despite having no formal training in perfume, Chong has successfully brought Amouage to a wider market. Since he joined the company he has launched nearly thirty fragrances, and he frequently travels to Grasse from the Middle East to work with perfumers there. He also introduced the Library collection, inspired by the idea of treasures in a library; each fragrance has a code or 'opus' number,

Gold for Men and Women, 1983

Ciel for Men and Women, 2003

Memoir for Men and Women, 2010

Lyric for Men and Women, 2008

Reflection for Men and Women, 2006

Honour for Men and Women, 2011

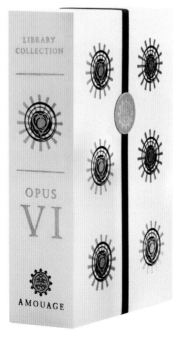

Opus VI, 2012

Opposite, left: A myriad colours and sizes of perfume bottle are encased in one large Amouage flacon, in a recent advertisement for the company.

reflecting its status as a work within a greater collection.

Chong's first fragrance for Amouage was Jubilation 25 Woman (2008), devised with the perfumer Lucas Sieuzak to celebrate the company's twenty-fifth anniversary. Chong considers Honour (2011) to be one of his most unusual creations. 'It was inspired by the last aria in the final act that Madame Butterfly sang to her son. The name was taken from the aria; if one couldn't live with honour, one would die with honour', Chong explains. 'The fragrance represents the evolution of Madame Butterfly's character from innocence and purity at the beginning to the final tragedy of betrayed love, which ended her life. I decided that all my creations should be related to one another, rather than creating one fragrance one year, which is entirely irrelevant to the one before or next. All my creations are linked by a narrative, which continues from perfume to perfume.'

Jubilation 25 Man, 2008

Angela Flanders

I have never wanted to sell all over the world; people come to find me from all over the world, in search of something special

Angela Flanders

Angela Flanders is one of London's most unusual independent perfumers. She started her almost doll's-house-sized perfume business from a small shop on Columbia Road, east London, in 1985. It is open for only five hours a week. Despite her understated, uncommercial approach, the entirely self-taught perfumer has built up a loyal and discerning clientele that includes many stars of film, television and theatre, although – with her trademark reticence – she is reluctant to name them.

Flanders took to the creation of fragrance as a secondary career in her early fifties. She was born in Buxton, Derbyshire, and studied fashion at Manchester College of Art before working as a costume designer for film and television. In the early 1980s she left to start working on interior-design projects, creating her own dried flowers

Figue Noir, 2006

and floral arrangements. She bought the shop next to a property she was renting on Columbia Road in east London, and began renovating it in Victorian style, opening in the spring of 1985. The boutique, which is close to the street's celebrated flower market, is open only on Sundays, the day the area (normally a quiet residential quarter) comes alive. The main room displays perfume, skincare products, candles and home fragrance, and a smaller room at the back contains shelves of essential oils. The building was a shoe shop in the late 1800s: for good luck, Flanders still keeps under the window a small shoe that was found during her renovations.

Flanders began her perfume journey as a creator of home fragrances, but one of her customers suggested that she make perfume. 'I thought I would have to make a range of at least five, but this client, whose mother was

Angela Flanders

Opposite: The Angela Flanders logo is inspired by an early nineteenth-century illuminated alphabet.

Opposite, left: Figue Noir (2006; top and bottom) and Rose Sauvage (2007). Flanders's candles are also extremely popular.

a famous perfumer, insisted that I had a knack for creating perfume and suggested that I started making some of my home scents for people', she explains. With that encouragement she went on to create her first perfume, Bois de Seville (1986), a spicy fragrance with orange, rose and bergamot, and notes of cinnamon, black pepper and clove; the long-lasting base notes are a compound of rare woods and balsams. Her next key fragrance was Coromandel (1988; now renamed Zanzibar), a woody fragrance evocative of east India and the Spice Islands.

It is full of cedarwood and exotic spices, with top notes of ylang ylang, jasmine and rose.

One of Flanders's key fragrances is Earl Grey (1994). It does not smell very obviously of the earl's famous brew, but there is a hint of tea and something else more romantic. It is an oriental scent, with a fresh bergamot top note layered over a complex rosewood heart. She also introduced dark, earthy base notes of patchouli and precious spices to give it a smooth, dry feeling. Another of her bestselling fragrances is Mint and Mandarin, which she developed

Above and right: The exterior and interior of the Angela Flanders shop on Columbia Road, east London.

in 1991 using green mandarin, bergamot and orange flowers; lavender and a hint of jasmine give it a lighter, softer touch.

In 2012 Flanders was honoured with one of the industry's highest accolades, the FiFi (Fragrance Foundation) award for best new independent perfume, for Precious One. She developed this scent of jasmine and tuberose, mixed with vetiver and oak moss, for her daughter Kate, who runs the fashion boutique Precious near by.

Flanders is selective about her ingredients. 'I started by making potpourri, and found myself with a lot of wonderful materials. I've been lucky to have had a supplier I trust, from the beginning.' She is also particular about the way her fragrances are made: 'I like to keep my patchouli for at least three months before I use it', she explains. The perfumes are sold in simple square bottles, packaged in bronze tissue paper and bags tied with black ribbon. Flanders also makes a range of bath products and lotions, and handmade candles in gold boxes.

Flanders has been approached many times by commercial firms keen to buy her out. 'So many people have come along who feel they could make some money out of me, but I never wanted to do that', she says. 'One of the liberties of working on your own is that you don't have someone breathing down your neck saying, "We need a perfume in the next three months". Perfume is an art form that needs time and space to be developed properly.'

In September 2012 Flanders opened a second shop, across the road from Precious, at 4 Artillary Passage, London. With its more conventional opening hours, it is a wonderful addition to her small empire.

Mille Fleurs, 1996

Precious One, 2012

Annick Goutal

Perfume is the music
of my dreams

Annick Goutal

In her brief lifetime, the perfumer Annick Goutal crafted intricate perfumes for an impressive clientele, ranging from the pop stars Madonna and Prince to the late Diana, Princess of Wales. This legacy has been lovingly continued by her daughter Camille Goutal and the perfume guru Isabelle Doyen, and now the brand has shops throughout the world as well as a flagship store in Paris.

Goutal (1945–1999) was the third of eight daughters. Her first talent was in music, and she began to learn the piano at the age of five. She excelled at the Paris Conservatoire, but in her twenties she became disillusioned with the demanding schedule of a concert pianist, and began to search for a more relaxed way of life. She worked as an au pair in London, where she was discovered one day when she was babysitting for the photographer David Bailey. He noticed her exceptional beauty and was the catalyst for her modelling career, which took her to Paris and Milan.

In 1976, after helping her godmother, Micheline Perrault, to make cosmetics and skin creams, Goutal by chance met a perfumer from the fragrance company Robertet in Grasse. She worked there for some time, developing the necessary skills for blending fragrances to make perfume, and in February 1980 she opened her first boutique, on the rue de Bellechasse, Paris.

The first perfume Goutal created was Folavril (1980), named after an antiques shop she had run in the late 1970s. An unusual fragrance, it contained tomato leaf with jasmine and mango for an earthy, spiced, oriental flavour. Very shortly afterwards Goutal created the outstanding Eau d'Hadrien (1981), one of her finest scents. It was inspired by Marguerite Yourcenar's novel *Mémoires d'Hadrien* (1951), a literary interpretation of the life of the Roman emperor. Uplifting and refreshing, the scent evokes the tanginess of citrus fruits and the shade of lemon trees. It has been extremely popular with both

Annick Goutal

Opposite: Eau d'Hadrien (1981) remains a classic. Its butterfly-topped bottle was designed by the artisan glass company Waltersperger.

Left: Hadrien Absolu (1987).

29

The interior of Annick Goutal's Paris store is decorated in pastel shades.

Nuit Etoilée, 2012

very last perfume she made was the touchingly named Ce Soir ou Jamais ('tonight or never'). Created only a few months before she died in 1999 at the age of fifty-three, and based on the concept of finding a rose in a priest's garden, it encapsulated everything she had learned about life: the passion, the beauty, the loss and the love. She left a legacy of twenty-five perfumes from her nineteen-year career.

In September 1999 Goutal's daughter Camille took on the role of head of the company and chief perfumer for the brand. Camille remains inspired by her mother: 'She tried to see beauty in every single thing: flowers, books, furniture, architecture, movies, music ... She always tried to see life in a positive way, even through hard times ... She kept telling me that honesty and generosity would make my life a better life. And she was right', she says.

Camille had worked as a fashion photographer, but she took up her new position with enthusiasm and began working with her friend and mentor Doyen, who is also a lecturer at the Institut Supérior International du Parfum, de la Cosmétique et de l'Aromatique Alimentaire (ISIPCA) in Versailles. Camille has developed the brand by creating fragrances that reflect her own style. She and Doyen have collaborated on Quel Amour (2002; a tribute to Camille's fiancé), Les Nuits d'Hadrien (2003; a more sensual version of the classic Eau d'Hadrien), Duel (2003; her first male fragrance), Mandragore (2005), the Les Orientalistes collection (Encens Flamboyant, Myrrhe Ardente and Ambre Fétiche, all 2007), Un Matin d'Orage (2009) and Ninfeo Mio (2009), among others.

men and women. She went on to make Rose Absolue (1984), an eloquent expression of her obsession with that flower.

In 1985 Goutal began working with Doyen, an established perfumer, on new scents. At that time the company was acquired by the Taittinger Group, which, by promoting it alongside other luxury-goods companies, its champagne house and the Baccarat crystal brand, allowed the perfumery to expand into shops all over the world.

In 1988, however, Goutal was diagnosed with breast cancer, and much of her work was put on hold. In remission in 1992 she returned to the company, and in 1996 another wave of creativity brought a new crop of perfumes, her final creations: Grand Amour, Eau du Sud and Petite Cherie. The

The perfumes' delicate packaging and the butterfly-topped bottles designed by the artisan glass-maker Waltersperger, based in Upper Normandy, have not changed since their inception.

In 2011, on the thirtieth anniversary of the creation of Eau d'Hadrien, Goutal and Doyen created Mon Parfum Cheri in memory of Annick, inspired by the glamour of the 1950s and based on chypre and patchouli. To honour the anniversary, Goutal created a limited-edition Eau d'Hadrien collector's bottle.

The company is now owned by the Korean beauty company Amore Pacific after Starwood Capital Group acquired it from Taittinger in 2005. Still head perfumer, Camille Goutal is now working on expanding the brand in the Far East and United States. With her innate sense of style, she carries on the tradition of beauty implemented by her mother.

Below, from left: Ambre Fétiche (2007); Myrrhe Ardente (2007); Encens Flamboyant (2007); Muse Nomade (2008).

Camille Goutal

All the bottles are made in Italy. Above, from left: Antonia's Flowers (1985), Tiempe Passate (1999; inspired by Bellanca's Italian grandfather) and Floret (1995). Each perfume is packaged with a stopper (left) and an individual spray.

In 2012, however, she started working on two new fragrances, one for men and one for women. She is particular about the standard and presentation of her perfumes, and refuses to allow any other company to do any online sales, in case they compromise on quality. Bellanca has never used advertising, and because the perfumes are available only in selected luxury stores around the world, she believes there is no need for it.

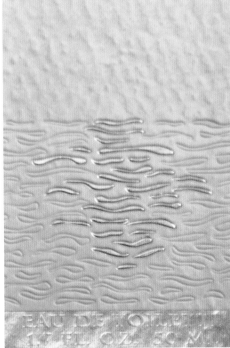

Above, left and centre: The pink packaging of Antonia's Flowers evokes the soft scent of the flowers.

Far left and left: Sogni del Mare was created in 2007, inspired by the sea and by nature. The packaging evokes moonlight on water.

Above and opposite: The flower on the packaging of Floret was created by the painter Dan Rizzie.

TIMBUKTU

Eau de Toilette

L'Artisan Parfumeur

Balance is achieved when opposites attract, like yin and yang. Nothing is lost or created, everything is transformed

Bertrand Duchaufour

L'Artisan Parfumeur, established in Paris in 1976 by the chemist and perfumer Jean-François Laporte (died 2011), is one of the first modern perfume houses to have embraced the concept of niche perfumery. Laporte's vision was to celebrate the finest ingredients and to move away from the global trends pursued by large companies. He wanted to go back to the roots of French perfume and highlight the work of the artisan, and to develop perfume that was poetic and romantic, bringing to the fore the emotions that fragrance inspires.

The company's first benchmark fragrance was Mûre et Musc, developed in 1978 by Laporte himself and still a bestseller, with its unusual combination of sweet blackberry and musk. The brand's other early scent that remains a classic is L'Eau d'Ambre (also 1978), an oriental fragrance with notes of amber, patchouli, vanilla and geranium.

It was created by Jean-Claude Ellena, who worked with L'Artisan on many perfumes, among them L'Eau du Navigateur (1982) and Bois Farine (2003), before he became the in-house perfumer for Hermès in 2004.

In 1983 Laporte sold L'Artisan, his second perfume house (he had established Sisley perfumes in 1972), to the international beauty company Cradle Holdings, and in 1988 he founded Maître Parfumeur et Gantier, a specialist perfume house and glovemaker. He went on to create Le Jardin du Parfumeur in Burgundy, a centre where visitors can discover the many fragrant plants, aromatic essences and spices that contribute to perfume-making.

L'Artisan Parfumeur has gone on to launch fragrances by such leading perfumers as Ellena and, more recently, Olivia Giacobetti (see p. 43) and Bertrand Duchaufour. Giacobetti hit the vein of

Mon Numéro 1, 2011

Bertrand Duchaufour

Opposite: Timbuktu (2004) and its exotic publicity images.

Right: The exterior of L'Artisan Parfumeur's Grande Boutique, 2, rue de l'Amiral de Coligny, Paris.

Right, bottom: The Valentine's Day 2012 display in the Covent Garden shop, London, featured oversized perfume bottles and hearts.

both unique and iconoclastic scents with her creation Premier Figuier (1994), one of the first fig-based scents. Its sharp and unusual fig fragrance has intrigued perfume enthusiasts. The warm and spicy African perfume Timbuktu (2004) by Duchaufour was inspired by a trip to Mali, where he observed the rituals of women dressing. In addition, Duchaufour – who has collaborated with L'Artisan Parfumeur since 1992 and also works with Penhaligon's (pp. 145–49; also owned by Cradle Holdings) – was responsible for Méchant Loup (1997), Poivre Piquant (2002), Dzongha (2006), Vanille Absolument (2009) and Nuit de Tubéreuse (2010).

The bottles of L'Artisan Parfumeur perfume emphasize the house's minimal design ethic. All are simple and rectangularly faceted, identical apart from the colour of the label and of the liquid inside.

As well as using well-established and experienced perfumers, the company is keen to promote new blood, and has taken under its wing such young perfumers as Anne Flipo, a graduate of the ISIPCA (the Institut Supérieur International du Parfum, de la Cosmétique et de l'Aromatique Alimentaire, Versailles) who worked with the master perfumer Michel Almairac and at the IFF (International Fragrance Foundation). Flipo created the groundbreaking La Chasse aux Papillons for L'Artisan in 1999, a fragrance rich in tuberose, jasmine and orange blossom. She also made Verte Violette (2000), with notes of iris, violet and violet leaf. Karine Vinchon, another graduate of the ISIPCA and formerly a junior perfumer at Robertet in Grasse, created Cœur de Vétiver Sacré

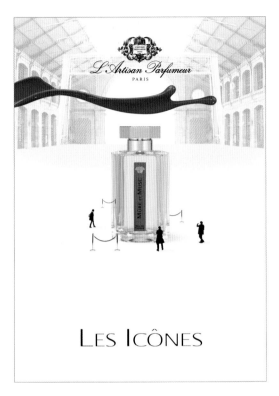

LES ICÔNES

POUR LUI

LES JARDINS SECRETS

Le nouveau parfum ardent

La Chasse aux Papillons, 1999

L'Eau d'Ambre, 1978

Mûre et Musc, 1978

Traversée du Bosphore, 2010

Nuit de Tubéreuse, 2010

(2010), a striking fragrance using vetiver from Haiti with notes of ginger and violet, white cedar, vanilla and musk.

There are now more than thirty fragrances in the company's range. L'Artisan Parfumeur also makes home-fragrance products, including Amber Balls, finely carved terracotta scented objects handcrafted by artisans in the historic region of L'Oise in northern France. Enclosed within each amber ball is a solid version of the warm, golden L'Eau d'Ambre scent, which is carried by currents of air and magnified by heat to radiate through the home over a long period of time.

From 2005 to 2007 L'Artisan Parfumeur enjoyed success in New York with four boutiques in Manhattan: a flagship on Madison Avenue, and others on Thompson Street, Fifth Avenue and Columbus Avenue. However, in 2009 the New York stores were closed. L'Artisan's flagship store is now on Place du Palais Royal in Paris, opposite the Louvre; there are stand-alone boutiques across the world, and the company is also represented in select department stores.

Jean-François Laporte helped to reinvent perfumery by taking it back to its roots. The garden he created in Burgundy still flourishes, as do the wonderful scents he created for L'Artisan Parfumeur.

Olivia Giacobetti

Olivia Giacobetti (born 1966) composed some of the most groundbreaking and iconic scents of the last century. She was one of the youngest perfumers ever to create a perfume for Guerlain.

The daughter of Francis Giacobetti, a photographer, Olivia was so inspired as a child by seeing Yves Montand play a perfumer in the film The Savage (1975) that she decided to devote her life to perfume. With the help of Annick Goutal (see pp. 29–31) she obtained an apprenticeship at Robertet at the age of seventeen, then studied at the Institut Supérieur International du Parfum, de la Cosmétique et de l'Aromatique Alimentaire in Versailles. She returned to Robertet in 1985 and remained there until 1990, when she founded her own production company, Iskia. At the age of just twenty-four she composed her first perfume, Petit Guerlain for Guerlain. Giacobetti has since created numerous perfumes for a range of bespoke houses, including Diptyque, L'Artisan Parfumeur, Hermès, Penhaligon's, Frédéric Malle, Lubin and Honoré des Prés.

Giacobetti was one of the first perfumers to champion the scent of the fig, and her creation Premier Figuier (1994) for L'Artisan Parfumeur ranks alongside Philosykos (1996), which she developed for Diptyque, as one of the finest fig-based perfumes.

In 2003 Giacobetti launched another brand, Iunx, with her father and Fabienne Conte-Sévigné, who – acting as artistic directors and consultants – have created the design, packaging and bottles. At first it was backed by Shiseido, but after three years Olivia gained full ownership, and went on to

develop further perfumes. With the aim of making Iunx the antithesis of traditional brands, she has created such unusual scents as blindingly white linen in sunlight (L'Eau Blanche, 2004) and a resinous fire (L'Ether, 2003); her range of candles includes Arbre à Pluie ('rain tree'), Papyrus and Fusain ('charcoal'). The first stand-alone store was on the rue de l'Université, Paris; now the boutique is attached to the fashionable Hôtel Costes on the rue Saint-Honoré.

Carthusia

When I first came to the Island of Capri ... and saw the beautiful Carthusia perfumery, I knew I had to make my life here

Michele Pagani

O n one of the most beautiful islands in the Mediterranean is one of the smallest niche perfumeries in the world. Perched among the luxury hotels, designer boutiques, al fresco cafes and whitewashed houses of Capri is a perfumery whose exclusive range of natural perfumes has been adored by the rich and famous, from Elizabeth Taylor to George Clooney and from Jacqueline Onassis to Penelope Cruz. Capri has attracted intellectuals, writers, artists and aristocrats over the years, including Compton Mackenzie, Graham Greene and the Nobel Prize-winning poet Pablo Neruda, who wrote many poems about the island. All were drawn to the island's beauty and idyllic nature.

The romantic legend of Carthusia goes back as far as 1380, when the father prior of the monastery of San Giacomo made a posy of locally grown flowers for the visit of Queen Joan of Anjou. When he threw the flowers away after three days, he noticed that the water that had held them had an incredibly beautiful fragrance. The monks recorded the combination of flowers that had been in the vase, distilled the water and produced the first Carthusia fragrance: Fiori di Capri. Once they had mastered the art of perfumery, they began to produce more scents, recording the details of each in a book. The monastery has been destroyed and rebuilt several times over the centuries, and the book of fragrance formulae was lost. During restoration in 1681,

Opposite: The company's logo, designed in 1984 by Mario Laboccetta, depicts a siren and flowers.

Left: Watercolour sketch of the monastery at San Giacomo, Capri, where Carthusia the perfumery was born.

Above: Perfumes are presented in a distinctive blue-and-white packaging.

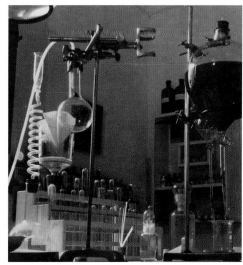

however, and after much searching, the book was found again, and production of perfume was restarted for a time. The name given to one of the company's most popular fragrances – 1681 (2010), which includes notes of tangerine, bergamot, coriander, lavender, petit grain, rosemary, thyme and musk – commemorates that event.

After a three-hundred-year break in production, the company's modern history begins in 1948, when a young Italian chemist, Dr Iovine, visiting Capri on holiday from Turin, was shown the old book of formulae by the prior. So enamoured was Iovine by Capri that he decided to live there, becoming immersed in the history of this charming island and its Carthusian monastery and creating a new laboratory to distil the unique aromas of Capri.

After 1950 Carthusia moved its factory from the San Giacomo monastery to viale Matteotti in the town centre, and during the

Opposite: The Carthusia store in Capri is hung with bunches of dried lavender.

Above: After 1950 the old production, as seen here in examples of early distillation, was moved to new premises in the town centre, on via Matteotti.

Many of the perfumes are today produced in Carthusia's laboratory on Capri.

Ligea, 2003

1960s and 1970s the company continued to produce some of the finest local scents. The Italian perfumer Laura Tonatto, who had previously worked for Armani, was brought in to reconfigure some of the classics and bring them back to life. In 1990, with her help, Carthusia's timeless fragrance Fiori di Capri, a delicious blend of carnation, sandalwood, ylang ylang and oak, was relaunched. Tonatto has also created perfumes inspired by characters from ancient myth, including the sirens Ligea and Io. Ligea (2003) is named for one of the three mermaids who tried in vain to seduce Ulysses. The warm scent of opoponax blended with the heady notes of mandarin gives it a spicy, seductive edge.

In 1998 the company was bought by a local businessman, Silvio Ruocco, who took over from Iovine. Ruocco installed Michele Pagani as general manager, and together they set about relaunching more of the brand's perfumes and creating even greater exclusivity. Carthusia continues to employ many of the methods used by the monks,

Mediterraneo, 2002

Fiori di Capri, 1390

Io Capri, 2000

1681, 2010

Io Capri, 2000

Capri Forget Me Not, 2012

Left, above and opposite:
Room fragrances and body
products are a recent
innovation by Carthusia.

hand-bottling and hand-wrapping every product at its small factory.

Via Camerelle (2005), a light scent made in homage to the fashionable street of that name in Capri, features refreshing notes of bergamot, lemon and bitter orange against a warm, herbaceous backdrop of marjoram. Aria di Capri (2003) is another of Carthusia's bestselling fragrances, with a floral bouquet of mimosa, iris and jasmine tempered by stronger notes of laurel and salty accents.

Many of the ingredients used in the perfumes are derived from local products. Rosemary is picked on Capri's Monte Solaro and is common to the men's fragrances, while the essence of the island's wild carnation is used in women's scents. Lemon and sage are also important. As production burgeons, Carthusia is now harvesting flowers from the area around Vesuvius on the Italian mainland, too. Each traditional apothecary-style bottle is handmade in Capri, based on those from the past but with a modern twist. The logo and label, designed in 1984 by the painter Mario Laboccetta, depict a 'flower siren' of a suitably mythical nature.

Since much of Carthusia's heritage is based on religion, the company has been careful to give due credit to the monks. It is currently renovating the prior's original garden, which carries much religious significance. In 2011 it sponsored a conference on the use of perfume in ancient cultures, in association with the University of Oriental Studies, Naples.

Carthusia currently makes fifteen fragrances; the latest is a scent of fig, vanilla and mint called Capri Forget Me Not (2012). It is a suitable tribute to the island to which this venerable perfume house owes its existence.

Clive Christian

My father always taught me that the way to recognize luxury is first to look at an item, and really decide whether you love it ...; only then, when you know you love it, should you look at the price

Victoria Christian

Few perfumes are marketed purely on their price. Yet the remarkable charisma and heritage that link the 'World's Most Expensive' perfume to its roots have ensured that it has a cult status among celebrities and royalty around the world. Queen Elizabeth and Prince Philip, Beyoncé, David Beckham, Goldie Hawn, Elton John and Serena Williams are just a few of the dedicated fans of this specialist brand. To own a bottle of Clive Christian's perfume is a luxury that many can only dream of.

Clive Christian, who was born in Dundee in 1951, originally designed luxury bespoke interiors and kitchens before taking over a small, ailing perfume house, Crown Perfumer, in 1999. In an unusual coincidence, as a young child many years previously his daughter Victoria had found a bottle of its perfume under the

Clive Christian

Victoria Christian

floorboards of the kitchen in their Cheshire home. Now Christian's No. 1 perfume (2001) has a place in the Guinness Book of Records: each fluid ounce costs £1000.

One of the main reasons No. 1 is so expensive is the high quality and rarity of its raw ingredients, and the fact that only 1000 bottles are produced each year. One ingredient is Rose de Mai, a rare rose that blooms for just three weeks in May (see p. 57). The essence is triple-extracted to make the absolute, each drop of which is made from 170 roses. Fifty-year-old Indian sandalwood is also used, as is Tahitian vanilla fermented for six months and crystallized to take on a softly spiced note of cherry liquorice. In the version for men, Indian sandalwood and Arabian jasmine combine to make a classic and unusual fragrance.

No. 1 Imperial Jubilee, 2001

Opposite: No. 1 (2001) is presented in a Baccarat crystal bottle with a diamond in the neck.

V, 2012

Christian then created 1872 (2001), named for the year in which the Crown Perfumer was founded and in which Queen Victoria granted the company the use of her crown's image for its bottle stoppers. In the version of 1872 for men, classic lavender and mandarin are mixed with clary sage to create a musky fragrance; the version for women combines lavender, rosemary, pineapple, patchouli and sandalwood.

X (also 2001) comes in a purple bottle and contains a particularly rare Egyptian jasmine, which is taken from the banks of the Nile at dusk, and orris, the root of the iris. The version for her contains peach and rhubarb; that for him has smoky notes of cardamom, ginger and amber. C (named for Christian's own initial) was launched in 2011; the version for women contains tuberose, violet, rose, jasmine and osmanthus, while that for men has notes of leather, sandalwood and spice.

Unsurprisingly, the packaging of the 'World's Most Expensive' perfume, No. 1, is exquisitely ornate. In the Pure Perfume presentation, the crystal bottle has a single white diamond in its neck. The award-winning No. 1 Imperial Majesty was made in an edition of only ten: seven were sold to private collectors; one is on permanent display at the Roja Dove Haute Parfumerie in Harrods, London; one is in Bergdorf Goodman, New York; and one is a world exhibition piece.

In 2011 Christian was commissioned to create a 'his and hers' monogrammed set of No. 1 perfume for the wedding of Prince William to Catherine Middleton. The bottles were presented in a black case with the royal coat of arms hand-embroidered inside. The

Above: Clive Christian produced a special limited edition of No. 1 for the Royal Wedding in 2011, with the initials C and W etched on Baccarat crystal bottles in a handcrafted box.

Opposite: Only ten bottles of No. 1 Imperial Majesty limited edition were produced worldwide, each costing £15,000.

CLIVE CHRISTIAN

1872, 2001

No. 1, 2001

X, 2001

perfume bottles are of hand-cut crystal embedded with a brilliant-cut diamond solitaire and etched in gold with a 'W' and a 'C' respectively. No. 1 is much loved among Hollywood stars, including Katie Holmes, who chose it for her wedding to Tom Cruise.

In 2000 Christian took a back seat in the company and allowed his daughter, a former West End musical performer, to take over as the ambassador for the brand. Although her father is still involved, Victoria now travels the world making people aware of the company's products. The perfume has a huge following in Russia, Dubai, China and the United States, as well as throughout Europe.

In 2012 Christian was awarded the OBE for services to the luxury-goods industry. It is an accolade that has cemented his position as a purveyor of classic British quality and luxury.

Victoria Christian

Rose de Mai

ROSA Cinnamomea Majalis.   ROSIER de M
F. J. R.

Rose de Mai has been one of the most outstanding natural ingredients of perfume for some time. It is taken from a rose that grows specially in Grasse and can be picked only in the first three weeks of May. It has a fresh and overpowering fragrance, which has captivated perfumers and perfume wearers for years.

Grasse's sheltered location and its rich mix of clay and chalk soils provide ideal conditions for flower-growing. Rose de Mai, a hybrid of *Rosa centifolia* and *Rosa gallica*, is harvested from the second year after planting. A single bush produces about 250 g of flowers; about 3000 kg of roses to 1 kg of Rose de Mai is a reasonable yield (about 170 roses to one drop of the absolute). The roses must be picked between 4 and 8 am, before the dew has evaporated from the petals, and are processed immediately.

A lighter rose essence with a fruity peach fragrance, Rose de Mai is also considered a top note. It is used in many perfumes, especially richly based ones by such classic brands as Clive Christian and Grossmith, which employ the absolute or triple-extract formulation. Roja Dove's Rose de Mai candle, which in 2012 won the Fragrance Foundation's award for the most outstanding new home fragrance, is one of the few candles to use real Rose de Mai (see pp. 157–61).

Creed

The dynastic perfume company Creed has been producing fragrances for more than 250 years. Its present-day clientele may range from Robbie Williams to Julia Roberts to Michelle Obama, but it was once the favourite of Queen Victoria and Napoléon Bonaparte. From father to son, the care and production of finely crafted scents have passed from the first owner to the current father and son, Olivier (born 1943) and Erwin (born 1980). Throughout the years, Creed has created more than 200 fragrances, many of which are among the present collection of about forty-five.

The house was established in London in 1760 by James Henry Creed, a tailor. Within just two decades of opening, it came under royal patronage with a commission from King George III, for whom Creed created the scent Royal English Leather (1781). Some time later, George V commissioned Royal Scottish Lavender (1856), a refreshing lavender-and-bergamot fragrance inspired by the Balmoral estate. It is still available today. In 1859, under royal decree from the Empress Eugénie, the wife of Napoléon and one of the firm's most devoted fans, Creed relocated to the 8th arrondissement of Paris. Eugénie loved many perfumes, and the scent the firm created for her in 1870, Jasmin Impératrice Eugénie, remains in the current collection. Other Creed patrons of the late nineteenth century included Emperor Franz Joseph I of Austria, his wife, Elisabeth, and Tsar Nicolas II of Russia. Further royal patronage was secured in 1885, when Queen Victoria appointed Creed 'official supplier' to the British royal court. That same year, Victoria was also the inspiration for the scent Fleurs de Bulgarie.

Not just lauded in royal courts, Creed was also favoured in political and celebrity circles: Winston Churchill was a devotee of Vintage Tabarome (1875), while John F. Kennedy

James Henry Creed (1710–1798)   Henry Creed (1765–1837)   Henry Creed (1824–1914)

Henry Creed (1863–1949)   James Henry Creed (1901–1980)   Olivier Creed (born 1943)

Erwin Creed (born 1980)

Opposite: Advertisement for Creed's Love in Black (2008). The perfume was inspired by Jacqueline Kennedy Onassis and created by Erwin Creed and his father, Olivier.

wore Vétiver (1948). In the 1940s, Fleur de Thé Rose Bulgare was created for the screen legend Ava Gardner. The fine, crisp, dramatic floral scent evokes the lush sensuality of the tea rose. Famously, in 1956, Creed made Flourissimo for Grace Kelly's wedding day: a rich floral fragrance that is still popular today, it has notes of bergamot, tuberose, Bulgarian rose, violet, Florentine iris and ambergris.

When Olivier Creed took the helm of the company in the 1980s, he re-established the brand's vitality with the creation of Green Irish Tweed (1985). 'This was an incredibly popular scent at the time,' explains Erwin Creed, 'a benchmark fragrance that has held great appeal'. It is a classic fougère fragrance, with top notes of iris and lemon verbena, heart notes of violet leaves and base notes of ambergris and

Jasmin Impératrice Eugénie, 1870

Royal Water, 1997

Right and far right: Creed was an award-winning tailor before its perfumes became world-renowned. Royal warrant from Queen Victoria dated 3 March 1885; royal warrant from Queen Maria Cristina of Spain, 1885.

Opposite, bottom, from left: Royal warrant from the Emperor of Austria, 26 March 1875; warrant from Napoléon III, 1870s.

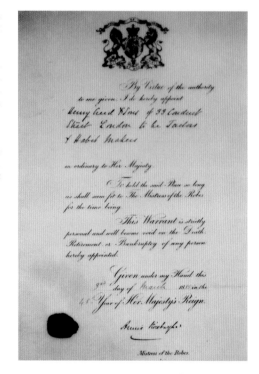

Tabarome Millésime, 2000

Original Vetiver, 2004

Fleurs de Bulgarie, 1885/1980

Fleurissimo, 1972

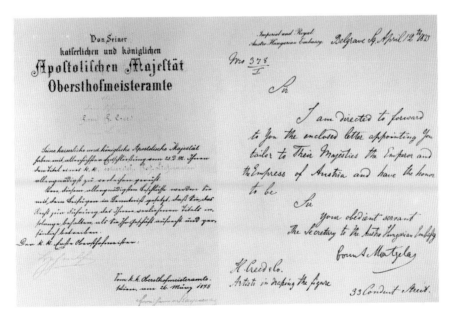

Mysore sandalwood. Olivier has designed many other classics, including Impérial Millésime and Silver Mountain Water (both 1995), Spring Flower (1996), Himalaya (2002), Original Vetiver (2004), Love in White and Original Santal (both 2005), Virgin Island Water (2007), Love in Black (2008), Acqua Fiorentina and Sublime Vanille (both 2009), Aventus (2010), and Royal Oud, Original Cologne and White Flowers (all 2011).

Creed does not employ outside perfumers or noses, but constructs the perfumes itself. The perfume historian James Craven, who works as an archivist for Creed, explains that Creed has remained such a cult classic brand partly because of its very high-quality ingredients. Another uncommon characteristic of the brand is that it still uses

Above: The interior of the Creed flagship store in Paris.

Above, right: The Paris store at 38, avenue Pierre 1er de Serbie has remained at the same location since Creed relocated to France from England in 1859.

Right and opposite: Advertisement for Green Irish Tweed (1985), one of Creed's most popular scents. The bottle is shown far right, with another popular fragrance for men, Bois du Portugal (1987). Tabarome Millésime (2000) and Impérial Millésime (1995) are shown opposite.

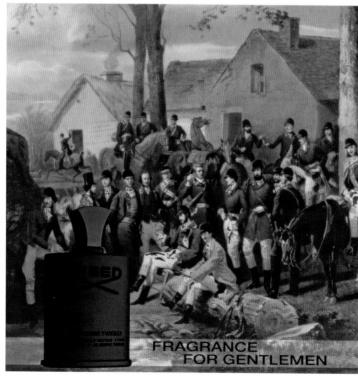

Spring Flower, 1996

Love in White, 2005

the traditional technique of infusion, a process now abandoned by many modern houses for being too expensive. 'This means that sometimes stock can take a lot longer to come in, and also [that] the prices are substantially higher', Craven continues.

In 2010, to comply with International Fragrance Association regulations, Creed stopped making many of its eaux de toilette. A number of ingredients had been banned and some were impossible to locate; now, only two of thirteen scents remain.

All bottles were made in the tradition of male scent-bottles, shaped like hip flasks, until 2001, when a more fluid, feminine shape emerged for the women's scents, engraved with the firm's crest. All these new designs were created by Erwin's elder sister, Olivia Creed.

Currently there are four Creed stand-alone boutiques in the world: New York, Dubai and Paris, where the latest opened in the 6th arrondissement early in 2013. Creed's perfumes are also available in department stores and independent perfumeries.

The family has always stayed close to its artisan roots, as Erwin Creed explains: 'We know our farmers. My father and I travel the world to select the best ingredients – the best bergamot, the best iris, the best roses. We meet the farmers and growers and choose our own selection.' Everything comes back to the workshop in Fontainebleau, south of Paris, where a small team of about thirty people creates the fragrances from blooms, buds, fruits, spices and woods. Even the bottling is done by hand. 'We have a family method, seven generations strong,' Erwin maintains. 'It works for us. It will not change.'

Creed also makes accessories and other products, including (from top) a brown leather atomizer; body lotion, shown here in the Love in Black fragrance; Fleurissimo deodorant; Silver Mountain Water (1995) candle; Green Irish Tweed shaving bowl.

Diptyque

At first renowned for its intensely scented candles, Diptyque now has range of nearly thirty fragrances, body products, room sprays and candles. The brand has attracted aficionados and collectors from the worlds of fashion, art and film: in 2003 the shoe designer Manolo Blahnik scented his entire exhibition at the Design Museum in London with Tuberose by Diptyque; Catherine Deneuve uses L'Ombre dans l'Eau; and Karl Lagerfeld is reputedly a keen fan of the Heliotrope and Pomander candles.

Although the name suggests a union of two people, Diptyque was in fact established by three artists in Paris in 1961: Desmond Knox-Leet (1923–1993), who had trained as a painter there; Christiane Gautrot (born 1926), who was a graduate of the École des Arts Décoratifs; and Yves Coueslant (born 1926), who studied painting at the École du Louvre. All three had designed fabrics and wallpaper for Liberty and Sanderson. They opened their first shop at 34, boulevard Saint-Germain, selling a selection of interior-design products, and to this day the shop stands at the same place.

In 1963 Diptyque produced the first three of its unique and now world-famous candles: Aubépine (hawthorn), Thé (tea) and Cannelle (cinnamon). The legendary standing of the candles today is attributed to the fact that they are hand-poured, which means that they retain a strong fragrance and last for a very long time. Each candle is said to take up to forty-eight hours to make.

As their candles gained in popularity, the trio decided to venture into the perfume world. The first Diptyque perfume was L'Eau, created by Knox-Leet in 1968. A spicy eau de toilette inspired by a medieval recipe, with notes of cinnamon, clove,

Opposite: Jardin Clos was created in 2003. It has top notes of watermelon and lilac blended with hyacinth and musk.

Above (left to right): Desmond Knox-Leet, Christiane Gautrot and Yves Coueslant in 1961 at the opening of the first Diptyque boutique, 34, boulevard Saint-Germain.

Left: The shop, which has not moved since it was opened, still has its original store front.

Vinaigre de Toilette, 1975

Do Son, 2005

Eau de Lierre, 2006

Eau Lente, 1986

Jardin Clos, 2003

L'Eau, 1968

L'Ombre dans L'Eau, 1983

Ofrésia, 1999

Olène, 1988

Oyédo, 2000

Philosykos, 1996

Tam Dao, 2003

geranium, sandalwood and rose, it aimed to capture the old-fashioned essence of an English aristocratic toilet water, with a French twist. From the inception of the company, the founders decided to maintain a consistent supply of their perfumes, so that if someone favoured a certain scent, they would always know it was available.

Knox-Leet was passionate about perfume: he bought ingredients from herbalists in Paris and England, brought back spices from his travels, and harvested special flowers and aromatic herbs, pounding his ingredients with a pestle and mortar, and infusing and dissolving them in paint pots to blend the perfumes.

As well as being the chief nose of the perfume house, Knox-Leet continued to paint throughout his life. Between 1983 and 1992 he held four exhibitions at the Galerie Varnier on the rue des Beaux-Arts in Paris, while the French president François Mitterrand not only used Diptyque candles but also had a painting by Knox-Leet hanging in his office. After Knox-Leet's death, Olivia Giacobetti (see p. 43), one of the youngest perfumers to have designed a perfume for Guerlain, was commissioned to create an enigmatic fragrance that would capture the scent of the fig, one of Knox-Leet's favourite fruits and evocative of the French countryside in the summer. In his honour, she created Philosykos (1996), which is now one of Diptyque's most popular scents.

Diptyque's simple aesthetic is embodied by its bottles, which feature the company's black-on-white logo and large black Bakelite lids. The lettering of the labels and

Above: The Diptyque boutique on Bleecker Street, New York, is lined with 180 hand-painted mirrors and hung with an artwork by the London-based designer Christopher Jenner.

Opposite: The company's simple bottles feature its instantly recognizable black-and-white logo and lettering based on the runes of an old Irish alphabet.

packaging, designed by Knox-Leet, is based on the runes of the ogham, an ancient Irish alphabet.

Diptyque has always maintained close links with fashion, and in 2003, with the designer John Galliano, it launched a candle that has a dense, deep, mysterious fragrance with no floral notes. Essence of John Galliano smells like burning wood, and has notes of vanilla and myrrh. The packaging for the candle is based on Galliano's own logo, the front page of an old English broadsheet newspaper with gothic lettering.

In 1997 a close friend of Knox-Leet, Mohamed Lataoui, became general manager of Diptyque, and he stayed with the company until 2005, when it was taken over by the private equity firm Manzanita Capital. Currently, Diptyque has shops in Paris, London, New York, Doha, Dubai, Hong Kong and San Francisco. Although the remaining two founders are now elderly, they are still involved with the development of the company.

In 2011 Diptyque commemorated its fiftieth anniversary with the launch of 34, a perfume that endeavoured to capture the smell of the boutique at 34, boulevard Saint-Germain using headspace technology, and which was formulated with the perfumer Olivier Pescheux. It is not as dramatic as some of Diptyque's offerings, with its light fougère scent that includes notes of blackcurrant, fig leaves, pink pepper, citrus, clove, cardamom, rose and balsamic. It is strikingly presented in a heavy glass bottled with a magnetic black stopper. It seems particularly appropriate that the Saint-Germain store should have its own scent immortalized in fragrance.

Floris

I capture smiles, giggles, laughter and tears when I create bespoke fragrances for Floris. Each is a unique and personal blend. What a privilege!

Shelagh Foyle

London's oldest perfume house, Floris, was established in 1730 on Jermyn Street by the Menorcan Juan Famenias Floris. It has become a uniquely trusted name among British perfumeries, supplying royalty, heads of state, film and television actors and musicians. Floris is also one of Britain's most traditional family businesses, and is still run today in the same location by descendants of the original family.

Edward Bodenham, currently the managing director of the company, is a ninth-generation Floris family man; he works with his cousin Polly Grindley at the Jermyn Street shop. His father, John Bodenham, and his uncle Christopher Marsh are the owners. Both are great-great-grandsons of Mary Anne Floris, who was the great-granddaughter of Juan.

Juan Floris began by selling a range of perfumes, combs and shaving products. In 1820 the company started to supply products to royalty, and since that time it has held sixteen royal warrants. The first is still on display at the Jermyn Street shop, alongside ledger books containing the company's first orders. Many perfumes were created exclusively for royal use. Special No. 127 (1910), a blend of bergamot and orange, was created for a Russian count in 1890 and named Orloff Special after him; it was introduced into the Floris range some years after his death, having been renamed to reflect the number of the page in the 'Specials' formula book on which the recipe was recorded. Admirers of the fragrance have included Eva Peron and Winston Churchill.

Whereas in its Victorian heyday Floris attracted the cream of European royalty, today its clients are more likely to come from Hollywood, with such stars as Liv Tyler, Joan Collins and Michael Caine among its devotees. Marilyn Monroe was a regular client in the 1950s, and had bottles of Rose Geranium rushed to her at the Beverly Hills Hotel in Los Angeles.

At first all Floris products were manufactured on site in Jermyn Street, but since 1989 they have been made at its factory in Devon; the glass bottles are handmade in Milan. The packaging has altered slightly over the years. In the 1970s and 1980s its classic navy with gold-embossed lettering was instantly

Juan Famenias Floris

Limes and Rose Geranium, two of the earliest Floris fragrances. Limes, the refreshing citrus scent, was created in 1832 and is still popular today.

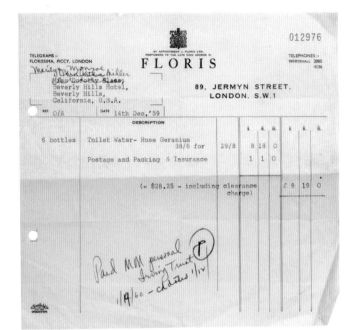

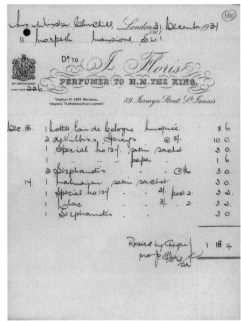

recognizable; in 2000 a design overhaul increased the spacing between the letters and gave each perfume box its own colour.

Stepping into the Mayfair shop is like going back in time; each piece of furniture has its own history. The wood-panelled salesroom contains Spanish mahogany showcases that were acquired from the Great Exhibition of 1851. At the back of the salesroom is a museum-like space that houses all the different bottles, boxes and equipment that have been used in Floris perfumes. This space is now the studio and laboratory of perfumer Shelagh Foyle, who joined the company in 2006, having previously worked for Yardley, Robertet and Givaudan.

To mark the 280th anniversary of Floris in 2010, Foyle created a limited-edition perfume called simply 280. Only 280 bottles of this oriental floral scent were made available worldwide. Among

Victorious, 2012

No. 89, 1950, aftershave balm

Right, top: Michael Bodenham, the great-grandson of Juan Famenias, works in the perfume cellar at the Jermyn Street shop.

Right, centre: The perfumer Shelagh Foyle has worked for Floris since 2006. As well as creating new fragrances, she also works on bespoke scents.

Right, bottom: The Jermyn Street shop features mahogany showcases from the Great Exhibition of 1851.

twenty other new perfumes, Foyle created Wedding Bouquet (2011) to commemorate the wedding of Prince William and Catherine Middleton. She has also developed the company's bespoke service. Floris now offers two levels of bespoke fragrance creation: one after a series of three ninety-minute consultations, the other after one consultation.

Although Floris continues to introduce new fragrances, some classics have been dropped, usually because of changing taste. The scents Lavender (1821) and Florissa (1978) have been discontinued; Floris has introduced Night Scented Jasmine (2006) and is working on a new lavender. 'It is very hard when we have to discontinue a perfume – almost like saying goodbye to a member of the family', explains Bodenham. Malmaison (1830), a heady mix of cloves and other spices, was recently withdrawn because it contained a higher concentration of cloves than is permitted by International Fragrance Association regulations. Stephanotis (1786) and Limes (1832), however, are still made today to their original formulae.

Floris fragrances are widely available in shops around the world, but the only place outside London in which the brand has ever had a stand-alone store is New York, on Madison Avenue in the 1980s. In October 2012, after nearly 300 years at the same shop, Floris opened a second London boutique at 147 Ebury Street in Belgravia. 'You could say we like to take our time about things', explains Bodenham with a smile.

Above: The Private Collection is Floris's most prestigious range.

Left: The brand has had its home at 89 Jermyn Street since 1730.

Frédéric Malle

I see myself as a publisher or editor of perfumers, or even a record producer: producing the best from my artists

Frédéric Malle

When you are the grandson of the founder of Christian Dior perfumes, your mother is an art director for Dior, and you share a birthday with the central character in Patrick Süskind's novel *Perfume* (1985), perhaps it is inevitable that you go on to play a pivotal role in the perfume industry. In fact, Frédéric Malle (born 1962) is one of the most critically acclaimed perfumers of the twenty-first century. Yet he has not created his perfumes single-handedly; like a star spotter or a diamond dealer, he has picked the ultimate perfumers to help him build his range, Editions de Parfums.

Malle trained at Sotheby's in New York before embarking on a degree in fine art at New York University. Although he had a passion for art, perfume was running through his veins: 'I remember people talking about perfume in my house as if it was a very serious subject. My mother always asked my brother and me what we thought of different types of smell, different types of packaging', he recalls. 'She used to wear a lot of the classic Dior scents, Miss Dior, Diorissimo – those are the earliest scents I remember. And when you begin

with Miss Dior, you end up doing Portrait of a Lady', he says of the perfume he created in 2010 with Dominique Ropion for the Editions de Parfums range.

After completing his degree, Malle worked at the Roure Bertrand Dupont laboratory in Argenteuil, France, and subsequently as a fragrance consultant for the fashion houses Christian Lacroix, Chaumet and Hermès before establishing his own company in 2000. Malle is disarmingly honest about how he created his brand. Without the enormous budgets for international advertising campaigns and the A-list celebrity endorsements available to large fashion houses, he used the one asset he was born with and has always maintained: unrivalled connections. 'All these people are my friends. Most of them come from the same laboratory', he explains. 'The idea for Editions de Parfums came from me, yes, but it also came from all these perfumers telling me they were bored of doing the same thing over and over again.'

For the Editions de Parfums collection, Malle worked with some of the outstanding perfumers of the time. He was inspired by

Frédéric Malle

Jean-Claude Ellena

Sophia Grojsman

Michel Roudnitska

Dominique Ropion

Opposite: Jean-Claude Ellena, Angeliques sous la Pluie (Editions de Parfums; 2000).

Jean-Claude Ellena
Bigarade Concentrée, 2001

Dominique Ropion
Carnal Flower, 2005

Jean-Claude Ellena
Cologne Bigarade, 2001

Dominique Ropion
Geranium pour Monsieur,
2009

Pierre Bourdon
Iris Poudre, 2000

Jean-Claude Ellena
L'Eau d'Hiver, 2003

Maurice Roucel
Musc Ravageur, 2000

Michel Roudnitska
Noir Epices, 2000

Dominique Ropion
Portrait of a Lady, 2010

Maurice Roucel
Dans Tes Bras, 2008

Olivia Giacobetti
En Passant, 2000

Pierre Bourdon
French Lover, 2007

Edmond Roudnitska
Le Parfum de Thérèse, 2000

Ralf Schwieger
Lipstick Rose, 2000

Edouard Fléchier
Lys Méditerranée, 2000

Dominique Ropion
Une Fleur de Cassie, 2000

Edouard Fléchier
Une Rose, 2003

Dominique Ropion
Vétiver Extraordinaire, 2002

Below: The Paris boutique has scented columns, designed specially by Malle to allow the experience of each perfume enclosed in a glass space.

Below, right: Malle has chosen black, red and white packaging for all the scents. Books are shelved all around the space, so that it feels like a library and not just a perfume boutique.

the French publishing house Gallimard, which published some of the last century's most iconic writers, among them Jean-Paul Sartre and Marcel Proust. 'Many of my friends are [publishers],' Malle explains, 'and I realize that the relationship they have with writers is very similar to the one I have with perfumers. With some I keep quiet and let them do their own thing, as I suppose Gallimard did with François Mauriac; just check the spelling mistakes and have it printed. Musc Ravageur [2000], for example, by Maurice Roucel, is a fragrance I hardly worked on. With others, I had a much more hands-on relationship, because some people need a partner.'

Malle brought Michel Roudnitska, Bertrand Dupont and Jean-Claude Ellena together in one room, along with such unsung fragrance stars as Sophia Grojsman (the creator of the blockbusters Beautiful for Estée Lauder, 1985, and Eternity for Calvin Klein, 1988) and Ropion (Safari by Ralph Lauren, 1990, and Amarige by Givenchy, 1991), and commissioned each to make a unique fragrance of their own, with no marketing brief and with the best possible ingredients that money could buy – on a blank canvas. There are currently seventeen different fragrances in the Editions de Parfums range, including the intense Carnal Flower (2005, with Ropion), a heady tuberose; the distinctive Geranium pour Monsieur (2009, also with Ropion); and Le Parfum de Thérèse (2000, with Edmond Roudnitska; see opposite), an enigmatic fragrance with notes of leather, tangerine, cedar and vetiver.

The first Editions de Parfums shop in Paris, on the rue de Grenelle in the 7th arrondissement, was designed by Andrée Putman and Olivier Lempereur. It looks rather like a gentleman's library, with books by Stendhal and Gore Vidal lining the shelves, and Malle's signature 'smelling columns' (floor-to-ceiling glass tubes that allow the customer to experience a scent in complete seclusion). Huge refrigerators house all the perfumes, so that customers can sample the products almost as though they are in a laboratory. Today, there are three Editions de Parfums shops in Paris and more than fifty outlets and concessions across Europe, including in Liberty of London; Malle's line is also available in Russia, Japan, Australia and the United States (in ten Barneys stores across the country and one shop in Manhattan). One in four fragrances sold in Barneys' New York store is by Frédéric Malle.

Malle is an obsessive lover of scent, a man who, in the process of perfecting a new fragrance, lives with half a dozen versions, placing them at different points on his arms when he goes to bed so that he can judge after a night's sleep his precise impressions of each one. 'It sounds like a grotesque habit, but it has been successful for me every time', he says. Malle's perfumes are worn by many Hollywood stars, although he does not like to identify them: 'We don't give celebrities our perfume', he says; 'they buy it because they like it ... I just know what they smell like when I see them on the red carpet, and I smile.'

Edmond Roudnitska

Edmond Roudnitska (1905–1996) devoted his life to raising perfumery to the level of an art form. He was born in Nice to a Russian family and began his career in 1926 in the laboratories of the perfume manufacturer Roure, composing bases, before moving to DeLaire in Grasse.

Roudnitska created many landmark fragrances, including Eau Sauvage for Christian Dior (1966) and Rochas Femme (1944). With his wife, Thérèse Delveaux, he founded the laboratory Arts et Parfums in 1946. There he worked on special and unique scents, including one that he developed solely and exclusively for Thérèse's use, code-named La Prune. This unknown scent became a legend in the industry for its composition of hitherto unused watery notes, such as cucumber, melon and watermelon. In 1956 Roudnitska offered the perfume to Dior; the firm did not take it, but liked the idea, and commissioned him to make something similar. From this, in that same year, Diorissimo was born.

Ever the perfectionist, Roudnitska continued to work on La Prune, and he and his wife vowed to keep the formula secret. Frédéric Malle was intrigued, and in 2000, four years after Roudnitska's death, he persuaded Thérèse to give him the formula so that he could reissue this masterpiece as a tribute to Roudnitska. Malle released it as part of his Editions de Parfums range and called it Le Parfum de Thérèse in homage to Roudnitska's wife, who had worn it for more than fifty years. It has become one of the Editions' bestselling fragrances. Roudnitska also created Diorella (1972) for Dior, Eau d'Hermès (1951) and Grande Eau d'Hermès (1987).

Grossmith

If I hadn't found the family connection and developed a passion for perfume, the Grossmith name and its fragrances could have been lost forever

Simon Brooke

Once one of Queen Victoria's favourite perfume houses, Grossmith was relaunched in 2009 by Simon Brooke, the great-great-grandson of the founder, John Grossmith. Today, the products of the revived house are sold in hand-designed Baccarat crystal bottles in the Harrods Roja Dove Haute Parfumerie, Fortnum & Mason and exclusive perfumeries around the world.

Brooke was fifty-two when his interest in genealogy led him to discover that he was related to the founder of a leading perfume house. So fascinated was he by the connection that he and his wife, Amanda, decided to abandon their careers (as a surveyor and an accountant respectively) and begin the task of revitalizing one of the most sought-after perfume brands of Victorian times.

As soon as Brooke had uncovered the family link, he set about learning everything he could about the company, which had been founded in London in 1835. His research became an obsession, and for more than eighteen months he trawled through internet records, library holdings and old newspapers. During the course of his research Brooke discovered that Grossmith was the only English company to be awarded a medal at the Great Exhibition of 1851 for perfumes and essential oils. He also unearthed a distant cousin, who still had that medal as well as two battered leather volumes of formulae. Handwritten by John Lipscomb Grossmith, the son of the founder, and containing more than 300 recipes, these books had been rescued from the company's London office during the Second World War.

Grossmith throve during the 1890s, but the death of two Grasse-trained family members in the 1920s heralded a gradual decline in the company's fortunes. In 1940 its premises were destroyed by bombing,

Opposite: The three classic Grossmith scents, Hasu-no-Hana, Shem-el-Nessim and Phul-Nana, in their original packaging.

Far left: Amelia Eliza Brooke, née Grossmith, the great-great-grandmother of Simon Brooke.

Left and below: Vintage crystal bottle and boxes from the Grossmith catalogue of 1921.

Right: Betrothal was created in 1895 to commemorate the engagement of the Duke of York and Princess Mary of Teck (bottom, left and right).

and post-war austerity meant that raw materials of the quality Grossmith required were no longer available.

In 2007, after a chance meeting with the master perfumer Roja Dove at a lecture at the Victoria and Albert Museum in London, the Brookes became determined to reinstate the brand, and enlisted Dove's help to develop the products. On his advice, they travelled to Grasse to discuss with the perfumers at Robertet how they could best re-create the fragrances. Two years later, despite being complete newcomers to the perfume industry, with the help of their new connections the Brookes brought out their first three scents. They chose three of the brand's most famous old fragrances and re-created them as faithfully as modern legislation allowed (real musk, civet and castoreum now being illegal under both European Commission and International Fragrance Association regulations).

The rich and oriental Hasu-no-Hana, a long-lasting fragrance with notes of jasmine, ylang ylang, Rose de Mai, bergamot and

Far right: Grossmith still possesses its historical leather-bound formulae books.

Opposite, left: This bright poster depicting cherubs advertised Shem-el-Nessim in 1906.

Opposite, right: The medals awarded to the company feature Queen Victoria and Prince Albert (top) and various mythical figures. They were rescued from Grossmith's former office at 29 Newgate Street, London, after bombing in the 1940s.

Below: The sketch and prototype by Baccarat of the crystal flacon.

Opposite: The three Baccarat flacons in today's elegant style, as available at the Roja Dove Haute Parfumerie, Harrods.

orange, was first launched in 1888 and is available once more. The same is true of Phul-Nana ('beautiful flower' in Hindi), developed in 1891 and one of Grossmith's most revered scents. It has a sweet citrus burst followed by a rich floral heart and a sensuous vanillic, woody drydown. Shem-el-Nessim, the third re-creation, dates from 1906; named after an Egyptian spring festival, it has notes of heliotrope and vanilla.

Betrothal (1895) was originally created to celebrate the engagement of the Duke of York and Princess Mary of Teck, later King George V and Queen Mary. Its revival in 2011 coincided with the wedding of Prince William and Catherine Middleton.

The original names of many Grossmith scents were particularly exotic. Brooke believes this was because royalty – rich, influential and well-travelled – were the trendsetters and fashion leaders of the day. 'Perfumes provided the imaginative perfume buyer with a "virtual" means of being transported to exotic foreign countries (Japan, India and Arabia). People were fascinated by travel and foreign places at the time, but only the rich could actually afford to go there', he explains.

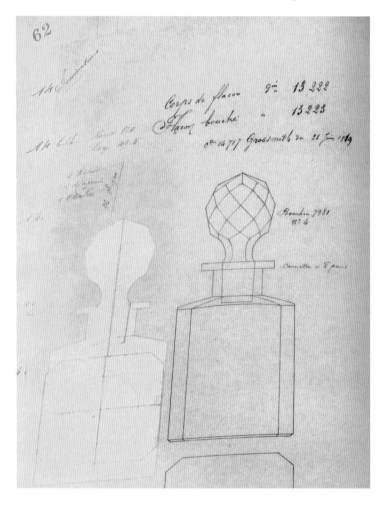

The Brookes pay equally close attention to re-creating the look of the original packaging. The bottle design for the Serie de Luxe range, which comprises the three classic scents, took its inspiration from a crystal flacon, 1000 of which were commissioned by Grossmith in 1919 from Maison Baccarat. The designers used a colour scheme of gold, white and regal blue, rather more subtle than the bright, multicoloured labels of the Victorian and Edwardian originals. Each bottle in the perfume range comes in a sumptuous white box, while the eau de parfum boxes are blue.

The rediscovered formulae books included recipes for nearly 100 different perfumes, soaps, essential oils and colognes. At present, Grossmith offers twelve perfumes, and the company looks set to expand soon. It certainly has no lack of inspiration for the future.

Betrothal, 1895

Hasu-no-Hana, 1888

Opposite: The bottles designed by Baccarat in 2009 for Shem-el-Nessim and Phul-Nana.

Below, left: The box that houses the three classic perfumes of the Serie de Luxe is closed by lock and key.

Hasu-no-Hana, 1888

Shem-el-Nessim, 1906

Phul-Nana, 1891

Houbigant

If God gave ferns a scent, they would smell like Fougère Royale

Paul Parquet

The perfume house Houbigant has an almost dynastic history, and has counted Marie Antoinette, Napoléon Bonaparte and many kings and queens among its dedicated followers. The roots of the company were first put down in Paris in 1775, when the twenty-three-year-old Jean-François Houbigant opened a fragrance shop '*à la corbeille de fleurs*' (at the sign of the basket of flowers) on the rue du Faubourg Saint-Honoré. He offered perfumes, pomades and scented leather gloves, a common combination at the time. One of the most intriguing legends attached to the history of Houbigant is that, on her way to Varennes in June 1791, Marie Antoinette made a detour to the shop and tucked three phials of perfume into her dress to give her strength to face the guillotine.

For nearly two centuries Houbigant enchanted the rich, the famous and the royal with its exquisite scents in stunning glass bottles, some of them designed by Lalique and Baccarat. There is even a receipt from Napoléon dated 17 May 1815, suggesting that he could have fought the Battle of Waterloo, exactly one month later, under the spellbinding scent of Houbigant. He commissioned perfume for his wife, Josephine, too.

In 1829 Houbigant was appointed perfumer to Her Royal Highness Princess Adelaide d'Orléans, the mother of King Louis-Philippe I, and nine years later the firm was awarded the licence of perfumer to Queen Victoria of the United Kingdom. In 1880 the house became even more influential when it came under the joint ownership of the perfumer Paul Parquet. Parquet moved operations from Paris to Neuilly-sur-Seine, just north-west of the city, so that the facilities could be expanded. The staff was increased, and laboratories were installed.

Elisabetta Perris

Opposite: A luxurious lilac box houses Houbigant's classic Quelques Fleurs Royale extrait (2004), in its pink bottle.

Left: Quelques Fleurs L'Original (1912).

Below: Quelques Fleurs limited edition in its sumptuous gift box.

Right: Houbigant advertisements from 1924 (left) and 1912.

Below, right: Quelques Fleurs compact, containing solid perfume.

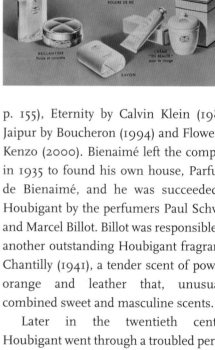

Two years later, in 1882, Parquet introduced Fougère Royale, the first male fragrance to incorporate a synthetic ingredient (coumarin). Parquet was the first to discover how to isolate such notes from raw materials. He continued introducing perfumes with synthetic ingredients, including Le Parfum Idéal (1900), Cœur de Jeanette (1908) and Parfum Inconnu (1910). Then, in 1912, another landmark was reached when the Houbigant perfumer Robert Bienaimé created Quelques Fleurs, one of Houbigant's all-time great fragrances and the first multi-floral scent ever made: it has strongly influenced many fragrances, among them Chanel No. 5 (1921), Joy by Jean Patou (1930), L'Air du Temps by Nina Ricci (1948), Fracas by Robert Piguet (1948; see

p. 155), Eternity by Calvin Klein (1988), Jaipur by Boucheron (1994) and Flower by Kenzo (2000). Bienaimé left the company in 1935 to found his own house, Parfums de Bienaimé, and he was succeeded at Houbigant by the perfumers Paul Schving and Marcel Billot. Billot was responsible for another outstanding Houbigant fragrance, Chantilly (1941), a tender scent of powder, orange and leather that, unusually, combined sweet and masculine scents.

Later in the twentieth century Houbigant went through a troubled period. In 1965 it was rescued by Enrico Donati, a prominent surrealist artist whose first wife was one of the last remaining descendants of the Houbigant family. He managed to revive the company's fortunes before ill health forced him to sell it to an Italian family, the Perrises (who also own Alyssa Ashley perfume), in 2005.

From their base in Monaco, brother and sister Elisabetta and Gianluca Perris and their father, Michele, have cleverly restored Houbigant's prestige. They reworked the famous Quelques Fleurs, re-creating the scent from the original formula and renaming it Quelques Fleurs L'Original (2009). It is a light floral scent, with fresh, warm, soft, powdery and sensual notes. Its many different florals include carnation, tuberose, heliotrope, orris and jasmine. 'The simple truth is that it transcends fashion and age', said the perfumer Roja Dove of the fragrance's success both past and present. To enhance its unique appeal, Elisabetta Perris, a fine-art enthusiast and business graduate, created a limited-edition bottle hand-painted with a flower.

In 2008 the Perrises consulted Dove, who was keen to help them re-create the hugely influential Fougère Royale. This, the first fougère perfume ever created, had established a completely new fragrance family, one that remains the most popular among men's scents. Dove advised them to approach Rodrigo Flores-Roux, head

perfumer at Givaudan, and Dove and Flores-Roux masterfully reworked the original formula to suit the modern world. The scent is a cocktail of lively citrus oils blended with an aromatic bouquet of lavender and geranium, which have become synonymous with fougère scents, and a floral, spicy yet fresh heart of Rose de Mai and clary sage with earthy, warming undertones. The original design of the bottle has been retained, but the overall look is more masculine and modern. The bottle's art-deco shoulders echo the spirit of the early twentieth century.

In 2012 Houbigant launched Oranger en Fleurs. This refreshing orange and rose perfume combines special ylang ylang from the Cormoros Islands and selected Turkish rose petals.

Houbigant has no stand-alone shops. Its perfumes, which are made in its factory in Grasse, are stocked by exclusive perfumeries and department stores around the world.

The iconic Fougère Royale (1882) is encased in a presentation box of black and silver (bottom). In the 1930s (left) it was advertised to the man who was 'willing to spend ... to begin each day with the luxury of a King'. An advertisement from 1948 (centre) simply emphasizes the fernlike scent, evoking its elegance and charm.

Jo Malone London

I don't consider myself
a perfumer – I consider
myself a fragrance artist:
I create art with scent

Jo Malone

Jo Malone established her eponymous label in 1994 in the bathroom of her rented London flat, with the aim of creating a line of simple, fresh fragrances and skincare products. Within months of opening her first shop, she had become known as a cult facialist and perfumer, and her unusual fruity and floral scents soon became the product of choice for such A-list clients as Stella McCartney, Kate Moss and Naomi Watts. Today, following an almost meteoric rise, Jo Malone London is a global luxury brand owned by Estée Lauder. Malone herself is no longer involved, but has begun a new independent brand, Jo Loves (see p. 99).

Malone (born 1964) was brought up on a housing estate in Kent and left school at the age of fourteen. Her father was an artist and magician, and at weekends Malone was his assistant. She remembers the smell of the white doves as she pulled them out of her father's hats. Her first job after leaving school was as a florist for Pulbrook & Gould in London. After a year's training, she went to work with her mother, a facialist (who had become seriously ill), and started developing her own range of products. After experimenting with oils, she decided to make her own ginger and nutmeg bath oil, and gave it to her regular clients as a Christmas present. So delighted were they that every one of them came back for more.

In 1994 Malone and her husband, Gary, a surveyor and a partner in her business, set up a shop on Walton Street, Knightsbridge. Within a week they had received an offer for the company, but Malone was keen to retain her independence. The brand grew beyond the couple's dreams, and within five months they had achieved the growth and turnover they had predicted would take five years.

English Pear & Freesia, 2010

Velvet Rose & Oud, 2012

Opposite: Advertisement
for the limited-edition scent
Plum Blossom (2012).

Malone, who has no formal training in perfume, worked with perfumers in Paris and Grasse to devise the unorthodox fragrances that have become her signature. Although there were doubts about such combinations as Nutmeg & Ginger (1990), these unusual scents have become some of the company's bestselling products, along with Grapefruit (1992), Vetyver (1995) and Amber & Lavender (1995). Originally used to fragrance a cream for massaging the arms, Lime Basil & Mandarin (1991) is Malone's most critically acclaimed perfume, and has become an icon of the late 1990s, referred to in films and books. It was conceived with the help of the perfumer Lucien Piguet.

The packaging for Jo Malone London's fragrances is instantly recognizable. Every bottle is exactly the same in design, with black-and-white lettering on a cream label, and is lavishly packed in black tissue paper in a box tied with a thick black grosgrain ribbon.

Malone has always pushed herself as far as she can. When she and her husband decided to take their perfumes to New York, they had no budget to develop the brand, just the products themselves. Malone wrote to one hundred people she knew in the city, including journalists, television hosts, friends and friends of friends, offering each of them ten of her products to pass on to their friends. The plan worked, and within months the brand was the toast of New York, with a shop on Madison Avenue and a concession in the luxury department store Bergdorf Goodman.

The company expanded rapidly, opening shops all over the United Kingdom and

Europe. In 1999 Malone accepted an offer from Estée Lauder to buy the company for undisclosed millions, but she remained a director until her departure in 2006. She was diagnosed with breast cancer in 2003 and took a year out of the business, returning in 2004 after making a full recovery.

Post-Jo, the Jo Malone London brand continues with Christine Nagel at the helm and creating the Cologne Intense range (2010), which includes Amber & Patchouli, Oud & Bergamot, Rose Water & Vanilla and Iris & White Musk. Nagel, a research chemist and market analyst, is now an award-winning perfumer; she also created Narciso Rodriguez for Her (2003) and Lalique's Encre Noir Pour Elle (2006).

Lime Basil & Mandarin, 1991   Blackberry & Bay, 2012

Jo Loves

In 2010 Jo Malone devised and sold to the BBC *High Street Dreams*, a television series offering advice on how to get ahead in business. During this time, she realized she wanted to create another perfume business, and a year later, in 2011, Jo Loves was born. Begun as an internet-only company, it is growing rapidly and looks set to be another success. Jo Loves offers nine scents, inspired by people Malone has met and places she has visited; Pomelo, Green Orange & Coriander, Orange Tulle and Gardenia

Jo Malone

were launched in 2011, and the Mango Collection, three scents on the theme of mango (below), in 2012.

Krigler

Perfume ... is a dream. From the person who grows the flowers, to the person who puts it into the bottles, everything must be done with love and happiness

Albert Krigler

Krigler fragrances have neatly epitomized the exclusivity of the niche perfume house for more than a century. With only two shops in the world – one in Monte Carlo and the other in the luxurious Plaza Hotel, New York – they have appealed to a distinguished clientele, including such film stars as Marlene Dietrich, Audrey Hepburn and Grace Kelly, who even inspired some of the fragrances.

Started in 1904 by the chemist Albert Krigler (1858–1955), the company has always been run by the same family. Krigler moved to Moscow from Berlin in 1872, and in 1879 created his first ever perfume, Pleasure Gardenia 79, as an engagement gift for his wife. The couple moved to St Petersburg, where Krigler started the company, before returning to Berlin in 1905. There Krigler had a laboratory and a small shop in the Victoria Hotel, where he sold his perfumes. The Kriglers started going to France, particularly the south, drawn by the favourable climate and by Albert's interest in perfume ingredients. They bought a small house outside Rheims, and called it Château Krigler, the name Krigler gave to one of his most renowned scents (1912), one that was worn by Grace Kelly. It was a revolutionary perfume for its time, being light and floral, made up of lily of the valley and mimosa.

In 1914, now ensconced on the Cap d'Antibes and with a perfume laboratory near by, Krigler created Lieber Gustav 14, inspired by a love letter of his daughter; it has the scent of amber, leather, black tea and lavender. The writer F. Scott Fitzgerald was one of its early devotees, and wore it while staying on the Côte d'Azur. Marlene Dietrich was another fan of this scent, confirming its unisex appeal. In 1919 Krigler created English Promenade 19, inspired

Albert Krigler and his wife

Opposite: Krigler perfume bottles are quintessentially elegant. These are on display in the shop at the Plaza Hotel, New York.

Left: Manhattan Rose 44 (1944; relaunched in 2005).

by the Promenade des Anglais, Nice's famous walkway. Some years later, when Audrey Hepburn was filming *Monte Carlo Baby* (1953), she visited Krigler's studio and was offered this fragrance, which she was said to adore.

Albert would remain in France until his death, but in the 1930s the Krigler perfume house moved to New York when Albert's granddaughter Lea married an American businessman. Before settling in upstate New York, they stayed for some time at the Plaza Hotel, where they began selling Krigler perfume. In 1967 Albert's great-granddaughter Kri Kri took up the reins and started her own laboratory in New York. Travelling between there and France, she focused on creating bespoke perfumes while reformulating a few of the brand's classics.

In the 1970s Krigler stopped producing commercial perfumes, as no one in the family was able to work on them, but in 2005 Albert's great-great-grandson Ben Krigler took charge and began to revive the company. Having studied architecture at the University of Pennsylvania and the Paris-Belleville School, he used his training to help with the design of the company's products and shop interiors. 'I've always been involved in Krigler, since I was a child. I grew up surrounded by perfumes. While others were playing with Lego, I was playing with perfume bottles. I started really being involved in the company in 2000. Then in 2005, at the age of twenty-five, I took control of everything', he explains.

Krigler set about re-establishing some of the classic fragrances, such as Château Krigler 12, Lovely Patchouli 55 (1955) and America One 31 (1931), which was worn by

America One 31, 1931/2005

Oud for Highness 75, 1975/2008

Château Krigler 12, 1912/2005

Blue Escapade 24, 1924/2010

President John F. Kennedy, among others. Cleverly, the formulae had been written in Cyrillic to prevent them from being copied by others, and kept in a safe. Krigler stayed as close to the original formulae as possible, but had to substitute certain ingredients, such as animal essences, to comply with modern regulations.

The company has recently introduced new perfumes. In 2009 it launched Extraordinaire Camelia 209, paying tribute to Krigler's favourite flower. In 2010 it developed Jazzy Riviera 210 to celebrate the 100th anniversary of its laboratory in Cap d'Antibes. Two years later it celebrated the centenary of Château Krigler 12 by making an even more luxurious version: Ultra Château Krigler 212 is made from the same formula as the original but fortified with rich magnolia, iris and freesia. Krigler is currently working on plans to open new stand-alone boutiques in Los Angeles, Las Vegas, London, Paris, Singapore and Berlin.

The Krigler bottles are labelled with the number of the year in which they were created, and each has a navy ribbon around its neck. Seen here are Relaxing Verbena 29, Juicy Jasmine 30 and America One 31.

Lorenzo Villoresi

When people come to me to ask me to make a perfume for them, I don't ask them questions – they tell it all to me. I'm more like a medium through which to channel the perfume they would like to have

Lorenzo Villoresi

On the top floor of a Renaissance palazzo overlooking the River Arno in the heart of Florence, amid leather-workers, goldsmiths and dress-makers, lies the perfume studio of Lorenzo Villoresi. Villoresi's creations have charmed world leaders and rock stars alike, from Jacqueline Onassis to Tony and Cherie Blair to Sting, who once commissioned Villoresi to make a birthday perfume for Madonna.

Villoresi (born 1956), originally a philosopher and student of ancient history and philology, possesses an air of old-world authority. His talent for perfume-making has been widely recognized, yet he is entirely self-taught. Born into an aristocratic Florentine family, he set out to be an academic, specializing in Hellenic studies. While at university he travelled to the Middle East, a journey that awakened his interest in perfume. He was overwhelmed by the scents and smells of the market-places in Marrakesh, Dar es Salaam and Cairo, and the amber-scented cigarettes and fragrant teas fed his imagination. At first just as a hobby, he used to bring back his own potpourri from his travels as gifts. A friend of a friend showed his potpourri

to the director of the Italian fashion house Fendi, who was immediately struck by his strengths as a perfumer and invited him to make products for Fendi's home collection. At this point Villoresi realized that he was perhaps not just a philosopher but also possibly a gifted perfumer.

At first Villoresi worked on bespoke fragrances, often spending hours with his clients in order to create their special perfume. Then, in 1990, he started his own company as a serious venture. Fortnum & Mason was one of his first stockists in the United Kingdom, and it remains one of the few, alongside Harrods and the specialist perfumery Les Senteurs.

In 1993 Villoresi created his first two commercial perfumes. Uomo (man) has strong elements of sandalwood, oakmoss and peppers. Designed for the 'perfect gentleman', as Villoresi describes it, the scent contains essences of patchouli and vetiver bourbon for a softer edge. Donna (woman), which was launched in

Lorenzo Villoresi

Opposite: Villoresi's bottles are all made in Tuscany, Italy.

Left: A travertine marble jar containing Villoresi's own blend of potpourri.

Above: Every essence is close at hand in Villoresi's studio in Florence.

Above, right: Lorenzo Villoresi works in his rooftop studio overlooking the River Arno.

Theseus, 2011

1994, is a soft, floral scent, mastered with a mix of Bulgarian rose and Rose de Mai from Grasse. It also has fresh, spicy notes of coriander, clove and star anise, as well as blackcurrant, violet leaves and jasmine.

Villoresi went on to create his own interpretations of many perfume classics. Acqua di Colonia (1996), his version of a classic cologne, is a strong, refreshing scent redolent of bergamot, sage, lemon and rosemary. In that same year he created his own versions of musk, patchouli, sandalwood, incenses, spices, vetiver and wild lavender. He has also developed his own, more unusual combinations. Fuelled by the images and scents of Greek myth and legend, his perfumes Dilmun (2000), Iperborea (2010) and Theseus (2011) all have a spicy edge. He now has more than twenty-five fragrances in his collection, all of which are supplied in glass bottles made in Italy.

Far left: Villoresi's studio extends to several rooms in his former home in Florence, each a sanctuary for perfume.

Left: Lorenzo and his wife, Ludovica, his muse and associate in his perfume business.

Below (left to right): Yerbamate (2001), Dilmun (2000) and Piper Nigrum (1999).

With his razor-sharp academic mind, Villoresi also lectures on perfume and has written books on the subject: *Il Profumo: Storia, Cultura e Tecniche* (1995) and *L'Arte del Bagno* (1996). He also edited and wrote the introduction to *Il Profumo nel Mondo Antico* (2010) by Giuseppe Squillace, which claims to be the first Italian translation of *De Odoribus*, a fourth-century treatise on scents by the Greek philosopher Theophrastus. In 2006 he was the first Italian to be awarded the François Coty Perfumer Award, one of the most prestigious international prizes for perfume.

Villoresi's next project is to create an Academy of Perfumes, which will include a museum of fragrance and an aromatic garden to provide education and training on the world of fragrances. Anyone can have their own bespoke perfume created by Villoresi, although there is a waiting list. He says he likes to remain accessible and helpful to others in passing on the art of perfume.

Above, left: Villoresi's home collection includes highly scented incense.

Below: Alamut (2006), in its distinctive red packaging, is a unisex fragrance.

When Villoresi first started making perfume he used only blue bottles, as this colour was traditionally used in pharmacies and helps to protect the fragrance from sunlight. He introduced frosted white glass with Teint de Neige in 2000. Red was used for Alamut in 2006 to reflect its sensual oriental fragrance.

Lubin

Holder of the beauty secrets
of the French Court

Gilles Thevenin

One of the first perfumers in Europe was Pierre-François Lubin (1774–1853), founder of the house of Lubin, who started his career as an apprentice before being made assistant perfumer to Jean-Louis Fargeon, personal perfumer to Marie Antoinette. In 1798, after the queen's death, Lubin opened his own shop in Paris, producing the formulae he had learned from Fargeon. The boutique was known as '*au bouquet de roses*', in honour of the late queen's favourite flower. In 1815 Lubin renamed the shop '*aux armes de France*', in a bid to reflect the ruling Bourbon dynasty. The shop attracted a glamorous clientele, including Empress Josephine, the wife of Napoléon Bonaparte, and Pauline, Napoléon's sister, who later became Princess Borghese. So indebted was Lubin to her patronage that he created a scent especially for her, Pauline (1809).

In 1821 Lubin received royal approval by becoming the official supplier to the British king George IV; in 1823 he also became the supplier to Tsar Alexander I of Russia. In 1830 he gained the title of official perfumer to the French royal court through Maria Amalia (the niece of Marie Antoinette, and the last queen of France) and her husband, Louis-Philippe I.

In 1844 the Lubin company was taken over by the Prot family, who retained control for more than a century, until 1960. The Prots aimed to bring the brand to a more international market. In 1873 they opened a modern factory in Cannes, where they championed the use of steam machines to produce the perfumes, and in particular to extract the oils. Lubin enjoyed success in the United States in the early nineteenth century, with stores in New York, New Orleans and St Louis.

As was the case with many perfume houses, the economic crash of 1929 badly affected Lubin's business. It still managed

Opposite: Black Jade (2011) was inspired by Marie Antoinette.

Above: The original shop, in Paris, was opened in 1798.

Left: The Lubin logo.

PARFUMERIE LUBIN — USINE DE COURBEVOIE

Above, clockwise from top left: Lubin factory, 1880; Lubin factory in Courbevoie, Paris, 1916; Lubin shop on the rue Royale, Paris, 1955; interior of Lubin factory in Cannes, 1924.

Right: Paul Prot (left) and André Prot, grandsons of Felix Prot, who bought the company in 1844.

Far right: Paul Prot in the laboratory at Courbevoie.

to produce perfumes, however, and in 1934 launched one of its best known perfumes, Nuit de Longchamp, inspired by a famous nocturnal horse race at the Parisian racecourse.

In the 1950s Lubin continued to sparkle; its style was epitomized by Gin Fizz (1955), which was created by the perfumer Henri Giboulet in homage to the film star Grace Kelly. By the 1960s, however, the brand's glamour was beginning to fade, and with no family member around to keep a stake in the company, it was taken over by a larger group. Thereafter it was sold several times, to French then German owners. By the end of the 1990s it was the property of Mülhens, a well-established perfume-maker from Cologne, and had lost much of its aura.

In 2004 Gilles Thevenin made a bid for the company. Thevenin had previously worked as a creative director for Guerlain and Rochas, but was a great admirer of the Lubin brand, and wanted to re-establish its position as a luxury niche perfume house. It took him six years to acquire the business, with the help of other investors.

Left: The motto 'Aux Armes de France' was adopted by Lubin in 1815.

Left, centre left: Princess Pauline Borghèse granted Lubin her official patronage in 1808.

Left, centre right: Record of orders from Empress Josephine, February 1809.

Below: Decorative vintage perfume labels from the company's archive.

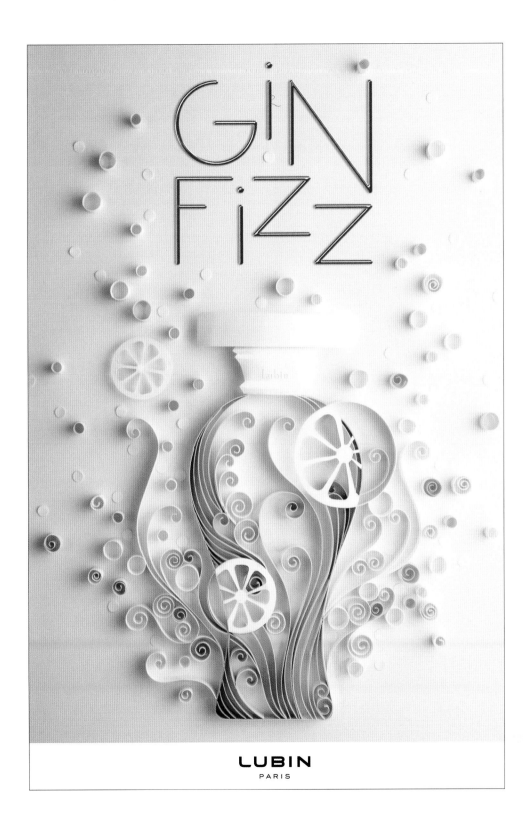

Opposite: The original bottle of Nuit de Longchamp (1954) and advertisement featuring a small dog with a bow on its head. The scent was reissued in a plain but elegant bottle in 2008.

Left and below: The iconic Gin Fizz was created in 1955 in homage to Grace Kelly.

Right: L de Lubin was created in 1975 by Lucien Ferrero and reissued by him in 2008.

Below, left and right: The captivating scent Idole de Lubin was created by Olivia Giacobetti in 2005.

Idole, 2005

He views Lubin's history with great admiration, and spent a lot of time researching it. 'I tried to change it back to what it was until the late 1950s, a very exclusive luxury French perfume-maker, with a worldwide distribution of high-end retailers', he explains. Lubin now employs just twelve people around the world, and its products are sold in selected shops, as well as from the flagship store on the rue des Canettes, Paris.

Thevenin has launched several new fragrances and reworked such classics as Gin Fizz and Nuit de Longchamp. In 2005 he commissioned the perfumer Olivia Giacobetti to work on Idole de Lubin, a new fragrance and Lubin's 466th scent since 1798. It commanded a great deal of attention for its clever combination of woody, smoky and leathery scents, and it has proven to be one of the brand's most sought-after new fragrances. Other perfumers who work with Lubin today include Lucien Ferrero and Thomas Fontaine. A few perfumes in the range were 'rebuilt' from old formulae: L'Eau Neuve, developed in the spring of 1968 by Roger Broudoux, was reformulated by Ferrero in 2007. It was inspired by Eau de Lubin, first created in 1798 and a favourite eau de cologne of Empress Josephine. In lovingly restoring and re-creating the brand started by the apprentice to Marie Antoinette's perfumer, Thevenin has created a contemporary cult appreciation of Lubin's perfumes.

FIGARO

LUBIN
PARIS

INÉDITE

LUBIN
PARIS

BLUFF

LUBIN
PARIS

ITASCA

LUBIN
PARIS

Left, clockwise from top left: Posters for Figaro (2010), Inédite ('unpublished'; 2009), Le Vetiver Itasca (2010) and Le Vetiver Bluff (2009).

Below: Le Vetiver was created in 2007 by Lucien Ferrero. As are many of Lubin's scents, it is housed in a slim, engraved glass bottle with a rectangular wooden stopper.

Maison
Francis Kurkdjian
Paris

Aqua
Universalis

Maison Francis Kurkdjian

Le Mâle (1995), the blockbuster scent he created for Jean Paul Gaultier at the tender age of twenty-five, propelled Francis Kurkdjian into the limelight. Six years later, in 2001, he became one of the youngest ever recipients of the François Coty Perfumer Award, one of the perfume industry's highest accolades.

Kurkdjian (born 1969) was drawn into the world of perfume almost by accident. He wanted to be either a ballet dancer or a tailor, but his glittering fragrance career was to be determined by his inability to dance or to make clothes. When he failed to get into the Paris Dance School, he opted for another passion, and applied to the Institut Supérieur International du Parfum, de la Cosmétique et de l'Aromatique Alimentaire (ISIPCA) in Versailles. He was inundated with work as soon as he had graduated, and his first project, the development of Le Mâle, met with great success. He worked with Acqua di Parma to create the stunning Iris Nobile in 2004, and was the mastermind behind Elizabeth Arden's iconic Green Tea (1999) and Lanvin's updated Rumeur (2006).

Kurkdjian has collaborated with a number of artists, perhaps most unusually

Francis Kurkdjian

capturing the scent of money for Sophie Calle. Calle gave him carte blanche, and the resulting perfume was revealed at the Soirées Nomades event at the Cartier Foundation for Contemporary Art, Paris, in 2003. For Kurkdjian it was an exciting project, but one he viewed in exactly the same way as all his other perfume briefs: 'I first looked for inspiration and gathered all my ideas until I had a clear vision of what I would create. An old $1 bill that had passed through many hands inspired me. It smelled like ink, paper and dirty fat. I was

> Being a perfumer is a bit like being a magician: it's about realizing your vision of someone else's emotions
>
> Francis Kurkdjian

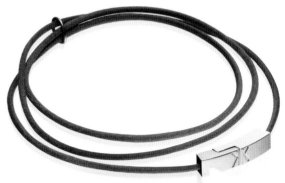

Opposite: Aqua Universalis (2009).

Above: Kurkdjian creates unique scented objects, such as scented bracelets, scarves and scented bubbles for children.

This page: The interior of the Paris store, on the rue d'Alger, was designed in collaboration with Fred Rawyler and Jean-Hugues de Châtillon.

Opposite, top: Kurkdjian uses theatrical window displays in his store. This gold-lit Eiffel Tower was created by de Châtillon.

Opposite, bottom: To celebrate the tenth anniversary of Kurkdjian's bespoke atelier, a limited-edition fragrance was presented in special crystal flacons.

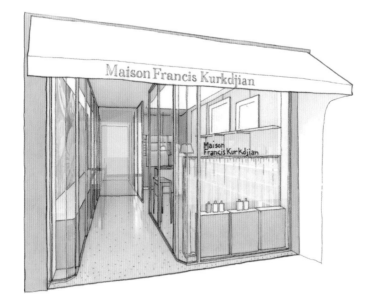

also inspired by expressions like "money has no smell" and "the smell of dirty money".'

Three years later Kurkdjian developed M.A. Sillage de la Reine, a re-creation of Marie Antoinette's signature scent, made by her perfumer Jean-Louis Fargeon. The fragrance was based on Fargeon's original formula, discovered by the writer Elisabeth de Feydeau during the research for her book *A Scented Palace: The Secret History of Marie Antoinette's Perfumer* (2006). It contained rose, iris, orange blossom, tuberose and jasmine, and was updated with grey amber and tonkin musk.

Before setting up his own perfume house, Kurkdjian travelled with a box of scents, rather like a portable mini-laboratory, to conjure bespoke fragrances. 'I travel most often to where my clients are, sometimes

at their home, sometimes in places where they feel comfortable and at ease, in an environment where they can express themselves with confidence', he explains. 'Trust is paramount to me, because without trust you can't create a custom perfume. It is actually a form of self-seeking.'

Kurkdjian believes that in creating perfumes he has found the best way to express himself. The establishment of his own house, Maison Francis Kurkdjian, on rue d'Alger in Paris in 2009 was a dream come true: 'I wanted my house to offer luxury in every detail. I also wanted the quality of service and product to be consistent, whatever the price. In *Breakfast at Tiffany's* [1961], Audrey Hepburn is looking to buy something from Tiffany's, but she has only ten dollars ... That is the spirit I was looking for in my house. I also had in mind the fine shops of old Paris. The colours of the city inspired me, with the grey zinc roofs and gold domes of the emblematic monuments of the city. Paris is the city of light.'

Kurkdjian worked with a team of young architects to shape the interior of the shop, and collaborated with the art director Fred Rawyler and the set designer Jean-Hugues de Châtillon to devise a vivid, theatrical space. 'Being a perfumer is about creating a memory that will last', he says.

Always keen to be unconventional, Kurkdjian has included in his range of fragrances such unusual products as Les Bulles d'Agathe, a range of scented bubble mixtures inspired by his young niece; scented leather bracelets; and perfumed laundry-detergent tablets. In 2012 he launched Oud, which uses the purest and most expensive oud from Laos. Enriched with woody and spicy notes of cedar, patchouli and saffron, it provides a dynamic accompaniment to Kurkdjian's other unusual scents: Acqua Universalis, APOM, Lumière Noire and Cologne pour le Matin and le Soir (all 2009).

Perhaps Kurkdjian's genius lies partly in his dissatisfaction with what he does. He may have created some of the most significant scents of the last century, but his real passion seems to lie in music and dance: 'I like to play the piano, at least three hours each day. Bach, Beethoven, it's never enough for me.'

Absolue pour le Soir, 2010

Absolue pour le Matin, 2010

Aqua Universalis Forte, 2011

APOM pour femme, 2009

Miller Harris

I love the smell of fresh rain first hitting the earth – that was the inspiration for my perfume Terre de Bois

Lyn Harris

Lyn Harris has a sense of smell that only a perfumer could live with: 'I can smell everything, the drains on the street, what someone has eaten for breakfast. As I get older it seems to be getting even more acute. It can be difficult for me travelling in certain places.'

Harris (born 1967) started the company Miller Harris in 2000 with the idea of creating only natural perfumes. (Miller is her father's middle name.) Today, as the only classically trained perfumer working in the United Kingdom, she has a global brand with three stores in London, and sells her products throughout the world, from Tokyo to New York. The black botanical print used on all the company's packaging was found by Harris in an eighteenth-century book of prints, and is instantly recognizable. Miller Harris was the brand chosen in 2010 by Samantha Cameron, wife of the British prime minister

Coeur de Fleur, 2000

David Cameron, as a gift for the American First Lady, Michelle Obama, to mark the Camerons' first visit to Washington.

Harris was raised in Halifax, West Yorkshire, and it was there as a teenager that she started working in a perfume shop, Irving Lodge, at the weekends. 'I loved perfume from the first time I could remember smelling my mother's Chanel No. 5 on her when I was about ten', she says. 'I started by making tea in the shop, but as time went on I gradually began serving the customers. I remember being in awe of it all. It was the days of Charles of the Ritz and Van Cleef. Jean Patou and Chanel were big, and Estée Lauder fragrances were becoming popular; a lot of people were buying Youth Dew [1953].'

Harris's earliest memories seem to have formed her taste palette. She spent her school holidays at her grandparents' home near Inverurie in Aberdeenshire, and remembers the smell of her grandmother's raspberry jam cooking on the stove. She claims that

Lyn Harris

Opposite: The botanical print on the Miller Harris label was discovered by Lyn Harris in an antique book of prints. She has used it throughout her packaging.

Fleur Oriental, 2000

Citron Citron, 2000

Terre de Bois, 2000

the way her grandmother lived her life – she baked her own bread, kept chickens and had a beautiful flower garden 'with every type of flower in it' – has provided inspiration for her own career: 'It was this kind of intense attention to detail, and living in an organic way, that inspired me to create my own perfume company.' Harris's philosophy is that smell is all about experience and memories. She believes that, day to day, you should never wear only one fragrance, 'because you will stop being able to smell and experience it. It's like wearing the same jumper every day. Instead, you should have a wardrobe of fragrances to suit your mood and outfit.'

Harris left school at sixteen with a great passion for perfume but few qualifications. She went to Paris, where she studied under the perfumer Monique Schlienger at the perfume school Cinquième Sens. Schlienger had been a pupil of Jean Carles (see p. 131), the iconic and eventually anosmic perfumer behind Carven's Ma Griffe (1946), among many other classic scents. In 1995 Harris went to Grasse to study with the master perfumer Richard Melchio at Robertet, the perfume house that currently manufactures all Miller Harris fragrances. 'When I first went to Grasse, the industry was depressed', Harris recalls. '[Perfumers] were trying to create things that were going to be winning formulae, and they continued to use synthetics.' Harris wanted to use only natural materials – 'I wasn't interested in learning how to make washing-powder smells or artificial fragrance' – and she pioneered the reintroduction of natural perfumes. After her experience in Grasse, Harris was inspired to start her own

L'Air de Rien (2006) was created in collaboration with the French actress Jane Birkin. The scent cleverly evokes the smell of nothing, yet – redolent of cigar and pipe smoke and the smell of old libraries – it has a magical quality.

perfume business, and in 2000 she did so, with a combination of savings and a government loan of £200,000.

Although Harris says she is always pleased when she hears of celebrities wearing her perfumes, she points out that 'we would never do a celebrity scent as such'. In 2006 Harris collaborated with the actress Jane Birkin to create L'Air de Rien, a clever play on the scent of nothing, with the aim of conjuring the enveloping aromas of old libraries and smoky tobacco pipes.

Today, Miller Harris has three shops in London, and its perfumes are available around the world. Harris is keen to open a boutique in Paris. In recent years the company has diversified into making teas and olive oils. Harris has also designed a range of wallpapers with Karen Beauchamp, a leading wallpaper designer. Each of Harris's stores is papered in a unique floral print, echoing the botanical print used in her packaging.

Harris also makes bespoke fragrances. Such perfumes have a starting price of £8000, and Harris has a waiting list of up to a year. On her wedding day in 2008, Nicola Moulton, the beauty editor of *Vogue* magazine, wore a Miller Harris fragrance created especially for her. Moulton recalls Harris's way of working: 'She made me three different fragrances and asked me to wear each one for a week. One of the special things about Lyn is not just that she is so well versed in perfume technique, she is also a great listener. I spent a whole day with her and she asked me a lot about my childhood, and holidays I'd been on. At the end of the day it felt as though I had been in therapy.'

Jean Carles

As Beethoven wrote symphonies without being able to hear any of the notes, one of perfume's greatest ever composers, Jean Carles (1892–1966), mastered many of his iconic scents without being able to smell them.

Carles was the first director of the Roure Perfumery School (founded in 1946), now part of Givaudan, and taught the art of creating perfume in a way that is still widely used today. He mentored many great perfumers, including Jacques Polges, who created several blockbuster scents for Chanel, and Monique Schlienger, who went on to train Lyn Harris of Miller Harris (pp. 127–31).

Carles was not born without a sense of smell, but became anosmic later in life. He managed to continue working with his son Marcel, who could interpret his ideas. He created many classics, including Tabu (Dana, 1932), Shocking (Elsa Schiaparelli, 1937), Ma Griffe (Carven, 1946) and Miss Dior (Christian Dior, 1947).

A pioneer of the use of the artificial scent styrallyl acetate, Carles went on to experiment with many aldehydic floral chypres. He developed a system of olfactive study, organizing raw materials by similarity and difference in two distinct charts, one for natural substances and one for synthetics. His method still forms the basis for the study of perfumery undertaken by students at Givaudan and other perfume schools. Carles left a legacy of unique scents, and paved the way for the perfumer artists of the future.

Nicolaï

Perfume is probably the most sophisticated creation one can make; it's very intellectual. It's the most valuable product of our spirit

Patricia de Nicolaï

An intellectual and a perfumer, Patricia de Nicolaï has found a niche for her elegant range of exquisitely designed fragrances in the mass market of French perfumes. It was undoubtedly in her genes to be a perfumer: as the great-granddaughter of Pierre Guerlain and great-grand-niece of Jacques Guerlain, she inherited a gilded, scented legacy. She has vivid memories of the fragrance of Chamade (1969), as her mother tested her cousin Guerlain's ground-breaking products before they were put on the market.

De Nicolaï (born 1957) was interested in chemistry before her passion for perfume took over. When she discovered the Institut Supérieur International du Parfum, de la Cosmétique et de l'Aromatique Alimentaire (ISIPCA) in Versailles, the first exclusive perfumery school, her fate was sealed, and she enrolled there in 1979. During the summer months she took jobs at Rochas and Robertet and worked in such aspects of perfumery as marketing and distribution, but it was soon apparent that her great talent was for the creation of fragrances.

After graduating, De Nicolaï worked at Lautier Florasynth in Grasse (a fragrance company where many esteemed perfumers honed their skills) from 1982 to 1984, then at Quest (an international fragrance manufacturer, which has since been bought by Givaudan). While working there she helped in the re-creation of Lancôme's Trésor (1990; originally 1952), among other perfumes. Trésor appeared after De Nicolaï left the company, and was latterly credited to the perfumer Sophia Grojsman.

In 1988 De Nicolaï left to pursue her own creations, and that year the high standard of her work was recognized when the French Society of Perfumers awarded

Patricia de Nicolaï

Opposite: Three 'Eaux Fraîches' from the Nicolaï range: L'Eau Mixte (2010), À La Folie (2012) and Chic (2011).

Left: The Nicolaï logo features a sketch of an old perfume distillation device.

her its international prize for best young creative perfumer for her debut fragrance, Number One (which she launched in 1989). This award underscored De Nicolaï's position as one of the leading female fragrance-makers of her generation. Yet it was not an easy environment in which to be working as a woman: 'It was all men, really, and men did not seem to value the creativity that women could bring to perfume-making', she explains. De Nicolaï established her own company in 1989, with her husband, Jean-Louis Michau (a former economist), acting as her business partner and manager.

Number One is undoubtedly De Nicolaï's benchmark fragrance. It was developed in the 1980s, when heady, blowsy white florals ruled, but is still a bestseller. The next notable perfume she created was the oriental scent Sacrebleu (1993), which created waves with its powerful notes of tuberose, vanilla and carnation. After that came Patchouli Intense (1996), a kind of throwback to the patchouli fragrances of the 1970s.

De Nicolaï finds inspiration in everything around her, from natural raw materials, food and markets to perfumes themselves. Her recent fragrance L'Eau à la Folie (2012) was inspired by the taste of mango. 'You have to be very careful, as generally French people do not like fruity fragrances. It took more than a year to construct the correct scent', she explains. By adding notes of mint, orange, lime, Egyptian jasmine absolute and juniper, she made the soft, luscious scent of mango into a deliciously fragrant stand-alone perfume.

Nicolaï remains a small boutique perfume company with eight shops, seven in Paris and one on Fulham Road, London.

Above: The Nicolaï store at 45, rue des Archives, Paris.

Right and opposite: Nicolaï bottles have an antique sealing-wax stamp on their necks and are packaged in cream-and-blue boxes, a colour scheme that is matched in the interior of the company's boutiques.

Among its many celebrated clients are Naomi Campbell, Isabelle Adjani and Françoise Hardy. Unlike many perfume companies, which outsource the manufacturing, Nicolaï keeps a close tab on every area of production, with its own factory in La Ferté-Saint-Aubin, near Orléans.

De Nicolaï has recently taken on the distinguished role of president of one of the world's leading perfume museums, the Osmothèque in Versailles. Founded in 1990 by Jean Kerléo, who had worked for Jean Patou and Helena Rubinstein, the museum houses about 2400 fragrances in its building on the campus of the ISIPCA. 'People travel for miles just to smell a perfume', De Nicolaï says. 'Maybe their grandmother had worn it, or a dear friend. It brings back the memory for them and creates special identities.' She started lecturing there occasionally, and was then asked to be president, a circumstance she describes as 'a great honour'. She believes that the heritage of the perfume museum is as valid as anything else in French culture: 'Perfume is ... as important a cultural and economic export as fashion. It's a notion of art, and when in the middle of the nineteenth century synthetic molecules appeared, perfumers were not only chemists or apothecaries, they became artists.'

Left: Kiss Me Tender (2010).

Opposite: Nicolaï also produces a range of room fragrances. Pictured here is Dansons La Capucine, inspired by a well-known French children's song. The yellow–orange capucine (nasturtium) has large, strongly scented leaves.

Ormonde Jayne

> My love for perfume began as a young girl, when my mother gave me a bottle of Madame Rochas. From that day on I have kept every single bottle of perfume I have ever used
>
> Linda Pilkington

Since she started her company, Ormonde Jayne, in 2000, selling exquisitely hand-crafted perfumes, body lotions and candles, Linda Pilkington has turned what began as a hobby into an international business. What makes her perfumes different from others, she says, is her approach: 'I look for flowers, resins, woods that no one else has thought of using. Everyone has sandalwood or cedar, but no one has a perfume from black hemlock. All the ingredients have to have an extraordinary beauty.' Her search for excellence in her ingredients has made her a sought-after perfumer with such celebrities as Yasmin Le Bon, Goldie Hawn, Will Smith, Elton John and Bryan Ferry.

Pilkington followed various careers before she was drawn to the perfume industry. Her thirst for adventure took her all over the world, including to Botswana and South America, where she ran a cattle ranch. Her introduction to the world of perfume came about by chance, when she bumped into an old friend in London while working for a Japanese agrichemical company. Remembering Pilkington's childhood skill for making candles, he asked her to create scented candles for his fine jewellery shop, a Chanel boutique, on Old Bond Street. Pilkington embraced the new venture wholeheartedly, and, after many weeks of hard work – and after spending almost all her life savings – she finally obtained Chanel's approval and secured a contract to make candles for the shop. She then approached the designer Anouska Hempel, who commissioned Pilkington to make candles for her hotels.

With growing confidence in her perfumery skills (entirely self-taught), and by now making perfume as well as candles, Pilkington took part in the Top Drawer design show in 1999. From that one show she received orders from Liberty, the Conran Shop and Selfridges. At that point, she recalls, 'I thought, maybe I can make a living out of this, as I obviously know what I'm doing.' She bought her own studio, obtained an alcohol licence for blending the perfumes, and chose a company name derived from the road on which she used to live in Primrose Hill, north London (Ormonde Terrace), and her middle name: 'I thought I couldn't call the company Linda Pilkington as it's far too unexotic-sounding for a perfume range.'

Linda Pilkington

Opposite: Tolu (2002); Ta'if (2004); Tiare (2009).

Pilkington's first shop, a tiny boutique nestled among bespoke chocolate shops and silverware merchants in London's picturesque Royal Arcade, is just steps from the designer parade of Old Bond Street. Customers are invited to have a 'perfume portrait' made to discover what suits their individual style; this entails evaluating single notes so that the consultant can recommend particular scents.

In 2012 the Ormonde Jayne range boasted thirteen perfumes: Ormonde Woman, Tolu and Champaca (all 2002), Osmanthus, Frangipani and Casablanca Lily (all 2003), Ta'if and Sampaquita (both 2004), Orris Noir (2006), Tiare (2009), and, in the men's range, Ormonde Man (2004), Isfarkand (2005) and Zizan (2008). Because only the finest ingredients are used, the cost of Pilkington's signature oils is higher than that of the oils used by many

Above and right: Ormonde Jayne's Sloane Square shop, 192 Pavilion Road, London. Inside, black glass and low lighting create an exclusive environment.

Opposite: The original Ormonde Jayne shop, in the Royal Arcade off Bond Street, London, opened in November 2001.

Page 143: Ormonde Jayne now makes a range of perfumes, candles and skincare products.

ORMONDE JAYNE
London Perfumery
WATCHCLUB
www.ormondejayne.com
ORMONDE JAYNE
12

Osmanthus, 2003

Orris Noir, 2006

Ta'if, 2004

Tiare, 2009

of her competitors. Tiare, for example, is based on the extract of a Hawaiian gardenia costing €30,000 a kilo. The gardenia is so rare that the flowers are grown and picked only once an order has been placed.

Pilkington maintains a hands-on approach, working on the shop floor of each of her stores every week. She particularly enjoys creating bespoke, unadulteratedly luxurious products. In 2010 she designed exclusively for Harrods a special dusting powder for the body using her Ta'if fragrance. The powder contains 24-carat gold and is encased in a black lacquered box, handmade by carpenters in Sheffield, with an embossed gold sliding lid. Wherever possible, Ormonde Jayne uses suppliers based in the United Kingdom.

Today, with two shops in London as well as concessions in Harrods and Fortnum & Mason, Pilkington's repertoire of scents is available throughout the world. The products are also stocked in the prestigious Mandarin Oriental hotel in Knightsbridge, London. Although she is approached each week by financial investors and strategic buyers keen to have a piece of her lucrative business, Pilkington has no intention of selling. 'I started Ormonde Jayne with a core philosophy of uncompromising luxury, and I would never give that up to satisfy investors who ultimately want profit margins and a quick roll-out strategy', she says. 'I would like to see Ormonde Jayne go global, but picking only fifty to sixty points of sale worldwide. It will help me to stay in touch with my customer, maintain the quality, provide a proper and caring service, and maintain our status as a respected British-owned perfume house.'

Penhaligon's

One of the things I love most about perfume is the myriad memories it creates ... these memories will never fade

Sheila Pickles

The quintessentially English brand Penhaligon's, established in 1870 by William Henry Penhaligon, a barber from Penzance, is one of Britain's oldest perfume houses. Penhaligon, who was born in 1837, was apprenticed to Humphrey Roberts, a hairdresser, at the age of fifteen. By 1861 he had set up his own business in Penzance, and a decade later he moved with his wife to London and started working with a Mr Douglas, who kept an exclusive hairdresser's and perfumery on Bond Street. Douglas also had the lease of the Hairdressing Gallery in the Hammam Baths on Jermyn Street.

In 1874 Penhaligon took over the lease of the baths and started to attract new customers keen to use his own range of hair products and perfumes. Hammam Bouquet (1872) is still made today, and is popular for its heavy scent of sandalwood, spice and Turkish rose, evoking the heavy, sulphurous atmosphere of the Turkish baths.

In 1880 Penhaligon entered into a partnership with a former colleague, a Mr Jeavons. When Penhaligon died in 1902, the business (no longer a partnership) passed from father to son, and when William's son Walter took over, the firm's popularity increased. Penhaligon's received an early accolade with a royal warrant from Queen Alexandra in 1903. The stylish Walter, who became Master of the Hairdressers' Guild in 1909, had worked closely with his father; he took over the laboratory, creating new hairdressing products and perfumes.

One of Penhaligon's aristocratic blends from around this time is Blenheim Bouquet, created in 1902 for the Duke of Marlborough. Inspired by Blenheim Palace in Oxfordshire, the ancestral home of the Marlboroughs, this iconic scent remains one of the brand's five top-selling fragrances. With its refreshing blend of citrus, lime, lavender and pine, it was the antithesis of the florals that dominated Victorian

Opposite: Penhaligon's shop in Covent Garden, London, at 41 Wellington Street. The many fragrances are displayed in walnut cabinets and on tables throughout the boutique.

Left: Elixir (2008).

Above: Penhaligon's shop sign at 20A Brook Street, Mayfair, London.

Above: Advertisement for Hammam Bouquet, 1917.

Above, right (from top): The shop at 33 St James's Street, London, was occupied by Penhaligon & Jeavons from 1891 to 1927; Penhaligon's staff are pictured on a day out in 1907 at the home of Walter Penhaligon in Worthing.

Sheila Pickles

perfumes, and proved popular with both men and women. Both Oscar Wilde and Winston Churchill wore Blenheim Bouquet.

In 1921, after Walter's death, the company passed to his son Leonard. In order to obtain extra funding for the business, Leonard went into partnership with the Smart brothers. In 1928 the shop moved to 25 Bury Street, and two years later Leonard retired.

Ellen Smart, who had joined the company in 1928 straight from school, continued to run it until she retired in 1953, when the business was handed over to staff. In 1964 manufacturing was transferred to the barber Trumper's on Curzon Street (a great customer of the brand), and Penhaligon's was bought by Ivan Bersch of Trumper's in 1971.

Very shortly afterwards, Sheila Pickles, a former literary agent and a friend and

former employee of the film director Franco Zeffirelli, bought the business and set about transforming what had been a few products left on a barber's shelf into an internationally known luxury brand. In 1975 Pickles opened Penhaligon's flagship store on Wellington Street in Covent Garden, London. Determined to learn as much as she could, she had taken a course in perfumery at a college in south London, where she met the perfumer Michael Pickthall. Together they created some of Penhaligon's outstanding fragrances.

A new direction for the company, and its growing reputation as a cult perfume house, were cemented by the introduction of the fresh floral fragrances Violetta (1976) and Bluebell (1978). These became instantly popular on account of their purity and their faithfulness to the scents of the flowers after which they were named. Bluebell has been a bestseller since its launch, with fans as diverse as Margaret Thatcher and Kate Moss.

In 1977 Pickles created Jubilee Bouquet to celebrate the Silver Jubilee of Queen Elizabeth II. The last perfume she developed for Penhaligon's was Quercus (1996), two years before she left the company.

During Pickles's last decade as managing director, Penhaligon's went through a turbulent period. For a time Laura Ashley held the reins, but it relinquished them in 1990. A private equity company, Cradle Holdings, took over in 2002; it also owns another important niche perfume house, L'Artisan Parfumeur (see pp. 39–43), and the two perfume houses shared the skills of Bertrand Duchaufour, a leading perfumer. Duchaufour has been associated with the birth of many

Amaranthine, 2009

Hammam Bouquet, 1872

Sartorial, 2010

Juniper Sling, 2011

Bluebell, 1978

Left: Penhaligon's has a small shop on Brooke Street, Mayfair, London.

Left, bottom: Take a perfumed journey in a Penhaligon's scented taxi, seen here outside the firm's Wellington Street store.

Opposite: Penhaligon's shop in the Burlington Arcade, Piccadilly, London.

scents, including Acqua di Parma's Colonia Assoluta (2003).

Duchaufour introduced unusual fragrances that went against Penhaligon's grain. His first, the tropical oriental Amaranthine (2009), is a twist on white freesia. Another of Duchaufour's creations, Sartorial (2010), was inspired by the Savile Row tailor Norton & Sons. Juniper Sling (2011), developed by Olivier Cresp, was a homage to London's gin houses. Cresp had previously been most widely celebrated for creating Angel (1992) for Thierry Mugler.

Under the directorship of its chief executive, Sarah Rotheram, and its head of marketing, Emily Maben, the company strives to blend tradition with modernity. Recent promotional activities have relied heavily on social networking websites to create awareness of the brand; the company also works closely with perfume bloggers. Penhaligon's has even trained five London taxi drivers to be brand ambassadors. According to Maben, scented taxis are a cheaper method of advertising than taking out a page in a glossy magazine; they are certainly more unusual.

The Penhaligon's fragrance bottle, an apothecary-style bell bottle with a bow at the top, is based on a design by William Penhaligon. It was originally sealed by waxing the stopper and securing it with ribbon; this method is no longer employed, but is referenced by the decorative use of the ribbon.

In the twenty-first century Penhaligon's has succeeded in keeping a loyal and trusting clientele as well as reaching new audiences in the Middle East and Japan. By sticking to its core English heritage, it has maintained its cult status.

ROBERT PIGUET

PARFUMS

Robert Piguet

Robert Piguet taught me
the virtues of simplicity,
through which true
elegance must come

Christian Dior

Although he was first and foremost a fashion designer, Robert Piguet's foray into fragrance proved to be his most enduring legacy. He did not live to see the effect of his perfumes on the world of fashion, however.

Born in Switzerland in 1901, Piguet was destined for a career in banking, but he moved to Paris at seventeen to learn about fashion. There he trained at Redfern, and then for ten years under the watchful eye of Paul Poiret. In 1933 he established his own fashion house, and he went on to train such leading designers as Christian Dior, Pierre Balmain and Hubert de Givenchy.

In 1944 Piguet met Germaine Cellier, at that time the only female perfumer in France. Cellier, a trained chemist and a close friend of the writer Jean Cocteau, had a creative approach to fragrance and cut a striking figure on the French perfume scene. The first in a legendary line of fragrances she created with Piguet was Bandit (1944), a musky, leathery scent with a scandalous image. Launched on the Paris catwalk with models dressed as bank-robbers, all in black with pistols, smashing bottles of the perfume on the ground, Bandit was not for the faint-hearted.

It was, however, Fracas (1948), Piguet and Cellier's third offering (after Visa of 1945), that really put Piguet's name on the map as a perfume manufacturer; it also gave Cellier the gravitas to go on and make perfumes for Nina Ricci. Fracas made an immediate impact and garnered a cult following on account of the almost over-powering intensity of its tuberose content. The name 'tuberose' refers to the plant's tuberous root system; it has a small, white flower with a practically carnal smell. As well as Indian tuberose absolute, Fracas contained Tunisian orange blossom absolute, French jasmine and Italian iris-root butter. Marlene Dietrich and Marilyn Monroe were said to wear it, and, more recently, Madonna, Uma Thurman and Isabella Blow have been fans of the reworked scent, which was launched in 1996.

After his death in 1953, the perfumes of Robert Piguet continued to be sold under the ownership of different companies, but when the quality began to fade the fashion house almost disappeared. In 1994 it was rescued by an American company, Fashion Fragrances and Cosmetics, which, with New Yorker Joe Garces at the helm, set

Robert Piguet

Opposite: The advertising
for Bandit (1944) evoked a
strong female character.

PARFUMS-PARIS

Above: Robert Piguet was one of the leading fashion designers of the 1940s; in 1944 he diversified into perfume.

Opposite: Futur, Cravache and Calypso are all classic Piguet fragrances that were relaunched between 1999 and 2007.

about rebuilding the brand and relaunching its once bestselling perfumes.

Although Garces is now firmly entrenched in the fragrance world and has a reputation as a leading perfumer, he trained originally as a printer and typesetter before working on a beauty magazine. Eager to revitalize the prestigious heritage of Robert Piguet, he began researching the fashion designer's background and even met his relatives in Switzerland. Garces approached the Swiss fragrance manufacturer Givaudan, which held the original Piguet formulae, and started working with the perfumer Aurelien Guichard to get to the heart of the scents. Guichard, who had previously worked for Azzaro, Kenzo, Gucci and Nina Ricci, had to take extra care to preserve the original scent of Fracas. Bans on various raw materials by the International Fragrance Association mean that few mid-twentieth-century perfumes would be permitted today in their original form, and Guichard faced the challenge of re-creating Cellier and Piguet's vision while updating it with non-allergenic materials. With its all-black bottles, the Piguet brand has a discreet, timeless look that quietly references its heritage.

In 1995, a year before its relaunch, Garces placed an advertisement for Fracas in the American magazine *Town and Country*, and was overwhelmed by the response. 'I focused on two fragrances, Bandit and Fracas, and decided to put them into *the* best stores, then I brought out the other classic, Visa, also one of our bestsellers. All our fragrances sold very well', he explains. The company went on to re-create all Piguet's original perfumes: Baghari (2005; originally 1950), Calypso (1999/1959), Cravache (2007/1963) and Futur (1999/1974). The reworked scents became very popular with Hollywood stars, and now many celebrities, including Kate Beckinsale, Sofia Coppola and Iman, often cite Piguet perfumes from the 1940s and 1950s as their favourites.

In 2012, some sixteen years after relaunching the first of the original perfumes, Fashion Fragrances and Cosmetics announced eight completely new Robert Piguet scents, five developed by Aurelien Guichard – Bois Noir, Casbah, Mademoiselle, Notes and Oud – and the Pacific collection (Blossom, Chai and Jeunesse). Garces describes the impulse behind the new offerings: 'We wanted to diversify our company, to make fragrances for different cultures. People have different tastes and cultures, all over the world. One fragrance does not fit everybody; we wanted to create fragrances that reflect that.'

Douglas Hannant, 2011

Bandit, 1996

Visa, 2007

Baghari, 2005

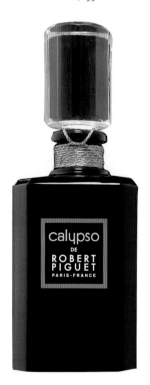

Calypso, 1999

Futur, 1999

ROBERT PIGUET
PARIS-FRANCE

Celebrate Elegance.

fracas
DE
ROBERT
PIGUET
PARIS-FRANCE

This advertisement was produced in 2008 to celebrate the sixtieth anniversary of Fracas, which was first made in 1948 by Piguet and Germaine Cellier.

Fracas

Once you have smelled Fracas, you will never forget it. Evocative of passion and style, it was beloved of Marlene Dietrich in its first incarnation, and still garners a distinctive celebrity following today, with aficionados including Uma Thurman, Madonna, Kim Basinger and Courtney Love. It also has huge cult appeal. It was created in 1948 by the French perfumer Germaine Cellier (1909–1976) for the fashion designer Robert Piguet, and was one of the first scents to incorporate the pungent aroma of tuberose. It also contains notes of jasmine, orange blossom, carnation and pink geranium.

It could be said that the secret of Fracas is the balance between the power of Cellier's style and the power of the tuberose. Cellier used the finest Indian tuberose absolute, which gives the fragrance great power and sillage (tenacity). She added a large quantity of Tunisian orange blossom absolute, plus French jasmine and Italian iris-root butter to give it a kick. The perfumer Aurelien Guichard is charged with the maintenance of the formula (a task that includes ensuring that all the ingredients adhere to current legislation), and he does so with an inspiredly light hand, allowing it to remain one of the outstanding scents of the last century. The name is the French for 'commotion', which is what the wearer of this passionate scent is sure to cause.

Roja Dove

One of the things I love about perfume is that it is not judgemental … it is not like fashion. Perfume can make the lady of eighty feel as though she is eighteen again

Roja Dove

Roja Dove is perhaps one of Britain's most high-profile and enthusiastic perfumers. Born and raised in Sussex on the south coast of England, he worked for Guerlain in London and Paris for twenty years before launching his own perfume range in 2007.

As a young boy Dove was fascinated by the perfumes belonging to his mother, whom he describes as 'an exceptionally stylish and social lady. She had a wonderful collection of scents; I remember she wore L'Aimant [Coty, 1927] a lot, and Shalimar [Guerlain, 1925].' These scents stuck in his mind, and, even as a medical student at Cambridge, he was intrigued by fragrance. A twenty-first-birthday trip to Paris, where he visited the Guerlain shop, increased his passion. Perfume, he decided, was to be his future.

Dove bombarded the head of Guerlain with letters asking for information about perfumes the firm no longer made. His interest was eventually acknowledged, and Guerlain offered him a job in the training and marketing department. After six years he gained the title of Professeur de Parfums, and later he became Guerlain's Global Ambassador, the first non-Guerlain family member to be given this honour. He worked at Guerlain for twenty years as a master perfumer, creating perfumes and training people in the art of fragrance. When the firm was taken over by the luxury-goods conglomerate LVMH in 2001, he decided it was time to leave. 'I knew the company was no longer part of a family firm', he says. 'A few months after I left, Jean Paul Guerlain also left.'

In 2001 Dove set up his own public-relations firm, RDPR, in his home town of Brighton, representing a range of clients in fragrance

Diaghilev, 2010

Roja Dove

Opposite: Amber Aoud (2012) is encased in a rectangular bottle, with a jewel-encrusted stopper. It is a bright and vivid statement perfume, and one of Dove's most popular.

and beauty. In 2004 the beauty guru George Hammer invited Dove to create his very own shrine to fine perfumes in Harrods. Called the Haute Parfumerie, it is a small, discrete space on the fifth floor, lined with panels that were originally designed for the Orient Express. Gathered here by Dove are exclusive, specialist perfumes, what he considers to be the finest fragrances in the world. He has also managed to persuade perfume houses to allow him to sell only specific parts of their collection. Here, many perfumes sell for £1000 or more per bottle.

In 2002 Dove was asked to create a perfume to be offered as a prize at a fundraiser for the Terence Higgins Trust. He cleverly decided to give a bespoke scent represented by an empty bottle, and asked Baccarat, the leading glass-maker, if he could use one of its finest examples. Brigitte Bury of Baccarat offered him the iconic blue bottle designed for Lubin's L'Océan Bleu by Georges Chevalier in 1925 for the Decorative

Arts Fair in Paris. Dove then fashioned a fragrance specially for the winner. 'When the partner of the winning bidder also commissioned me to make a perfume for them, that's when I thought I would invest in my own perfume range', he explains.

In 2005 Dove started his semi-bespoke range. Only fifty bottles of each perfume were created, and they were sold for about £1000 each in his Haute Parfumerie in Harrods. In 2007 he launched his Trilogy range with three key perfumes, Scandal, Unspoken and Enslaved. These perfumes were acclaimed for their strong themes – respectively, jasmine and tuberose; neroli and bergamot with an edge of jasmine; and ylang-ylang, rose and jasmine with carnation and an un-expected hint of patchouli – and were a great success. Dove went on to launch Danger (2011), a bright floral scent with notes of ylang-ylang, violet and gardenia; Risqué (2012), a leathery chypre fragrance warmed by jasmine, oakmoss and patchouli; and Mischief (2012), a fresh, green, citrus scent with galbanum and violet leaf.

In 2010 Dove created Diaghilev, commissioned to accompany the Victoria and Albert Museum's exhibition on the Ballets Russes; the stunning chypre, with its mix of orris, vanilla and vetiver, was made in an edition of just 1000, and sold out. The Middle Eastern fragrance Aoud was created in 2011, and Amber Aoud in 2012, a spicier, warmer version.

In 2012 Dove opened another Haute Perfumerie, in Lausanne, Switzerland. He also created a special fragrance for Queen Elizabeth II's Jubilee year, entitled Britannia, making sixty bottles to commemorate the sixty-year reign.

This exotic bottle for L'Océan Bleu by Lubin was given to Dove for his own perfume, beginning his career in the creation of fragrance.

Mischief, 2012

Danger, 2011

Risqué, 2012

In 2010 Dove curated an exhibition at Harrods, *The Perfume Diaries*, which neatly distilled the spirit of perfume from the early launch of Jicky (Guerlain, 1889) to the present day, while highlighting future trends. His work was recognized in 2012 with two FiFi (Fragrance Foundation) awards, one for his perfume Danger (in the category of best new fragrance in limited distribution), the other for his Rose de Mai candle.

Dove is ever the candid, charming gentleman. As he leaves the restaurant where we meet, I remark on how sweet he smells. 'Ah, it's just a little something I knocked up myself', he jokes.

Aoud, 2011

Scandal, 2007

Aoud Crystal Edition, 2011

ACQUA DI COLONIA RUSSA

OFFICINA PROFUMO
S. MARIA NOVELLA
FIRENZE
1612

Santa Maria Novella

She took on a new lease of life, frequently looking at herself in the mirror ... .
She used perfumes excessively; her linen reeked of vetiver, sandal, ixora, Peau d'Espagne

Júlio Ribeiro, *Flesh*
(1888, translated by William Barne, 2011)

The influence of the thirteenth-century perfume house Officina Profumo Farmaceutica di Santa Maria Novella has grown from simple medicinal herbs and potions created by Dominican monks to stand-alone boutiques in the upmarket shopping centres of America and the Far East; the company has also become one of the finest purveyors of high-quality perfumes and perfumed products in Europe. Santa Maria Novella, as it is usually known, is a cult artisan perfumer with its roots deep in religion, and began producing perfumed products in a Florentine building a few steps from the mid-thirteenth-century church of the same name. In 1320 the monks started using alcohol rather than vinegar or oil as a base for their scents, and in 1549 they created L'Eau de la Reine, the first world-renowned alcohol-based perfume, to celebrate the coronation of Catherine de' Medici.

Santa Maria Novella officially became a company in 1612, and passed to state ownership following the official confiscation of monastic assets in 1866. In 1871 it was ceded to Cesare Augusto Stefani,

the nephew of the last monastic director, Fra Damiano Beni. Stefani's family has run the business for more than three generations; now Eugenio Alphandery is the co-owner and general manager of the company.

In 1989 Alphandery, then an engineer, went to the firm's shop on Via della Scala to fix one of the machines. So shocked was he at the state of the company (which was facing liquidation) that he rescued it, taking over as general manager in 1990. He built a new factory in 2000 and has introduced new products, including more than fifteen perfumes. 'I realized the place was full of hidden treasures, and it seemed as though time had stood still ... It was a real pity that such historical beauty wasn't valued', he explains.

The key to Alphandery's success is his commitment to the firm's artisanal nature.

Opposite: Acqua di Colonia Russa (1901) is an intense citrus fragrance. Santa Maria Novella's labels have changed little over the years.

Above: The frescoed ceiling of the company's stunning saleroom on Via della Scala, Florence, was restored as part of the brand's 400th anniversary in 2012.

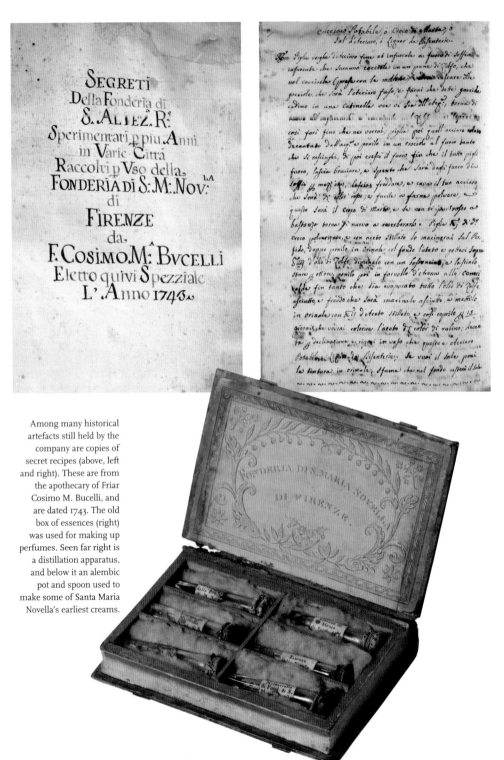

‘I didn't twist the artisan characteristics of the company’, he says. ‘I don't believe that a company [is] artisanal just because it has very few employees, [nor] that a company [must] be defined as non-artisanal because it has many employees. The products’ success comes from the unique way they are made.’ The firm uses technologically advanced machines and methods, yet many things are still made or finished by hand.

There are more than forty perfumes in Santa Maria Novella's current range. The brand's most renowned scent is Acqua di Colonia, also known as Acqua della Regina (‘the queen's cologne’), reputedly created for Catherine de' Medici on her marriage to Henry II of France in 1533. She brought this revolutionary citrus-scented perfume, with its sharp top notes of bergamot, with her when she moved to France.

Among many historical artefacts still held by the company are copies of secret recipes (above, left and right). These are from the apothecary of Friar Cosimo M. Bucelli, and are dated 1743. The old box of essences (right) was used for making up perfumes. Seen far right is a distillation apparatus, and below it an alembic pot and spoon used to make some of Santa Maria Novella's earliest creams.

Top: Adjoining the saleroom is a cabinet-lined salon displaying many beautiful pots and bottles. Here are sold herbal remedies, biscuits and pastilles, all bearing the Santa Maria Novella mark.

Above: The Olfattorio is a meeting room and special smelling area at the top of the building.

Left: The spectacular saleroom resembles a museum rather than a shop.

Other key scents are Muschio (1828), a strong musk, and Tabacco Toscano (2008), a smoky, leathery fragrance. The house's version of Peau d'Espagne (1901; originally produced in the eighteenth century) continues to charm; this spicy and rich, resinous concoction has been used since the sixteenth century to scent leather. Angels of Florence (2006) commemorates the floods that ravaged the city in 1966, and a donation is made to the charity of that name for each bottle sold.

The brand's spicy Melograno perfume (1965) was worn by Daniel Craig as James Bond in *Casino Royale* (2006), and the iconic perfumery was the backdrop to the film *Hannibal* (2001), starring Anthony Hopkins. More recently, the scents have been featured in the American television series *Gossip Girl* (2007–12). Aficionados of the brand include the actors Monica Bellucci, Penelope Cruz, Michael Douglas and Catherine Zeta Jones, the singer Gwen Stefani and the US Secretary of State Hillary Clinton.

Many of the perfumes were used in earlier times as household products. As early as 1381, flower waters were used as an antiseptic against the plague; the orange-flower water, Acqua di Fior d'Arancio, is still used for cleansing and toning the skin.

Potpourri is another iconic product for Santa Maria Novella; its version has a pungent, fruity scent that unfolds endlessly. If you travel by taxi in Florence, you will certainly smell its fragrance, since all the drivers carry a sachet of it. Soap is made with great care and attention, too, and hand-wrapped, to continue the artisanal feel. The milk soap is made from real cow's milk, not substitutes or powdered milk. The

Nostalgia, 2002

factory also produces candles, honey and Alkermes liquor, which is aged in oak barrels in the company's liqueurs cantina.

In May 2012 Santa Maria Novella celebrated 400 years since becoming a company with a glittering event presided over by the mayor of Florence. Its building was restored, with frescos and floors brought back to their Renaissance glory, and a commemorative stamp was introduced by the Italian postal service. Alphandery ended his speech at the party with the words, 'Let's just see if we can take it to the next 100 years!' There is no denying that the first 400 have been an overwhelming success.

Left: An antique bottle of Aceto da Toilette bears the label and logo that are still used today.

Opposite, left: Soap moulds, soaps and pastilles. The Vellutina soap (second from top) is said to give the skin a velvety texture.

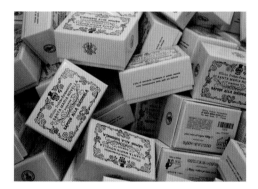

Russa, 1901

Melograno, 1965

Acqua di Colonia, 1533/1996

Serge Lutens

A fragrance is like a set of chords, not a series of harmonies; it is the emergence of a note, electrified by its collision with the following one; it is a chain reaction

Serge Lutens

Serge Lutens brings an almost magical dimension to his craft, concocting spellbinding perfumes. His idiosyncratic sense of style has ensured his status as one of today's most highly regarded perfumers.

Lutens (born 1942) originally trained to be a hairdresser in his home town of Lille, beginning as an apprentice at the age of just fourteen; two years later, however, he left to seek his fortune in Paris. His interest in photography developed, and he took some of his pictures to *Vogue*, where his talent was recognized by the editor, Edmonde Charles-Roux, who took him on. During the 1960s he worked with such leading photographers as Irving Penn and Richard Avedon on shoots, creating hair and make-up looks.

Christian Dior was so impressed by Lutens's *Vogue* portfolio that he commissioned him in 1967 to create a make-up line. A year later, Lutens went to Morocco, and decided to make his home in Marrakesh. It was the scents of that city that would eventually inspire him to become involved with perfume.

Lutens employed his many talents in various disciplines before immersing himself exclusively in the world of perfume. His fashion photographs were shown at the Guggenheim Museum in New York in 1973, and short films he made were screened at the Cannes Film Festival in 1974 and 1976.

In 1981 Lutens created his first perfume, Nombre Noir for Shiseido, made from chypre and white flowers and contained in a black octagonal Chinese bottle enveloped in intricately folded black paper. The black-on-black packaging, revolutionary at the time, was much emulated and generated a huge cult following. The perfume is no longer in production, and can change hands online for hundreds of pounds for even the tiniest sample.

Lutens continues to work with Shiseido, and in 1991 he opened his own flagship store in Paris, Les Salons du Palais Royal Shiseido, on the Place du Palais Royal. Nestling in a historic arcade, this luxurious boutique is as quiet and dark inside as a Renaissance church, with glass cabinets in shades of purple and blue. A spiral staircase leads up to a Japanese tea salon, where private consultations take place. Perfume enthusiasts travel great distances just to see

Serge Lutens

Opposite: Cuir Mauresque (1996). The company's logo is simple and striking.

the fragrances in their splendid home. Although many of Lutens's fifty-five perfumes are available online and in shops and concessions around the world, twenty-seven of them are available only in the Paris boutique, to ensure their exclusivity.

In 1992, a year after opening his flagship store, Lutens created another masterpiece, Féminité du Bois. This was his first female fragrance, and was inspired by the smell of wood shavings in a carpenter's workshop in the Atlas Mountains of north Africa. A rival perfumer has said that he would give five years of his life to have invented this perfume. Lutens went on to create Les Eaux Boise, a series of wood-based perfumes including Bois Oriental (1992), Bois de Violette (1992) and Chêne (the smell of oak; 2004).

Many of Lutens's perfumes are inspired by his love of Morocco. For example, the idea behind Iris Silver Mist (1994) – to create an iris scent so elegant and refined that it could be worn as easily by a man as by a woman – came to him while he was in a bookshop there. He collaborated with the perfumer Maurice Roucel to determine the ideal amount of iris.

Another perfumer with whom Lutens has collaborated is Christopher Sheldrake, who also works with Chanel. The two

In the Place du Palais Royal store (below) in Paris, an elegant spiral staircase (opposite) leads up to the private salon. Here bespoke consultations take place on low Japanese-style furnishings.

Tubéreuse Criminelle, 1998

Chêne, 2004

Iris Silver Mist, 1994

Ambre Sultan, 1993

developed Cuir Mauresque (1996), a rich, leathery fragrance that pays homage to Caron's Tabac Blond (1919). Another outstanding collaboration was Ambre Sultan (1993), a mix of coriander, sandalwood, bayleaf, patchouli, angelica, resins and myrrh. It has become beloved of fashion editors and film stars. Sometimes there is a violent edge to Lutens's perfumes; Tubéreuse Criminelle (1998) is said to have been inspired by a murder that took place in a room full of tuberose.

In 2000 Lutens launched his own brand, Parfums-Beauté Serge Lutens. For four consecutive years (2001–2004), he was awarded the FiFi (Fragrance Foundation) award for best original concept. He now spends all his time in Morocco. When he is not creating perfumes, he indulges in his other obsession, the restoration of an old palace in the Ben Youseff quarter of Marrakesh, not to live in – that would be far too conventional – but to observe. 'It will be a place for contemplation', he says.

Below (left to right): Perfumes from the exclusive range: Chêne (2004), De Profundis (2011) and Ambre Sultan (1993).

Right: Féminité du Bois (1992), an unusual mix of cedarwood, ylang ylang and musk, has become a classic for Lutens.

Niche Brands

Since the early 2000s there has been an explosion in the number of niche brands, reflecting a growing interest in the art of exciting, avant-garde and unusual cult perfumes. Not all these fragrances will stand the test of time, but each has its own distinctive idea and branding for the future.

Andrea Maack

Andrea Maack is an Icelandic fine artist whose intricate line drawings inspire and inform her perfumes. She graduated from Reykjavik School of Art in 2005 with a BA in visual arts, and worked in London and New York as a fashion buyer before launching her perfume company in 2011, with scents created for her exhibition *Eau de Parfum* (2010). Her unique process involves sending her drawings to her perfumer in Grasse, who interprets her work by creating a scent to match. She has created six very different perfumes: Smart, Craft and Sharp (all 2010), Silk and Dark (both 2011), and Coal (2012), the last of which includes actual elements of coal and was inspired by the smell of charcoal. Her perfumes are now sold all over the world.

Bond No. 9

The Bond No. 9 collection of eaux de parfum is inspired by New York City. The company, which was founded in 2003 by Laurice Rahmé, is named after the address of its headquarters and boutique at 9 Bond Street in NoHo. Its fragrances aim to immortalize iconic landmarks of New York and the surrounding area, or to celebrate the ethos of the city. Such perfumes as Gramercy Park (2003), Bleecker Street (2005), Fire Island (2006) and Brooklyn (2009) feature in its range of more than sixty fragrances.

Blood Concept

Blood Concept began in 2011 as a collaboration between the Italian copywriter and photographer Antonio Zuddas and the fashion designer Giovanni Castelli. Using blood and blood types as their inspiration, Zuddas and Castelli have stuck to metallic notes and have not used any florals at all in their collection of five perfumes. Their A perfume is green and aromatic with essence of tomato leaves and basil, while B is woody and spicy with notes of pomegranate and patchouli. The smoky O has notes of leather and thyme; MA evokes memories of childhood with its clean laundry notes; and AB is a synthetic mix of cedar and slate.

Byredo

The Swedish perfume house Byredo was founded in 2006 by Ben Gorham, who has an Indian mother and a Canadian father and grew up between New York, Stockholm and Toronto. In his twenties he played basketball professionally, then studied fine art at Stockholm School of Art. After graduating, he met the Swedish perfumer Pierre Wulff by chance and decided that he wanted to create scents for a living, rather than be a painter. He had no formal training, and so Wulff recommended that he work with two of the world's leading perfumers, Olivia Giacobetti (see p. 43) and Jerome Epinette. Gorham also uses some of the world's leading photographers for his packaging and design shots. The fragrances, which are now sold in more than twenty countries, are called such dandyish names as Baudelaire (2009) and Mister Marvelous (2011), along with the more classic La Tulipe and Oud Immortel (both 2010).

By Kilian

By Kilian is a line of niche luxury eco fragrances established by Kilian Hennessy, part of the family that owns Hennessy cognac. Hennessy first became interested in fragrance while studying at the Sorbonne; he went on to train at Firmenich in Switzerland, and worked for a number of well-known fragrance brands before launching his own line in 2007. By Kilian fragrances are supplied in refillable bottles in lacquer boxes with lock and key; the refills are sold separately. The idea is that if you buy one bottle, you will never need to buy another, as it can be refilled as often as is required. There are currently nineteen fragrances in four collections, and nine candles, sold from the flagship store on boulevard Haussmann in Paris.

Illuminum

The British perfume house Illuminum was launched in 2010 by Michael Boadi, a former hairdresser, and has thirty-two fragrances in its collection. Catherine Middleton sowed the seeds of its success when she famously wore White Gardenia Petals (2010) for her wedding to Prince William in May 2011. In just a few minutes this light, white floral fragrance became overwhelmingly popular; it sold out immediately, and was not back in stock for four months. Other fans of the brand include Michelle Obama, Leonardo DiCaprio and James Franco. The fragrances are divided into four groups: floral, citrus, musk and oud. Moroccan Tuberose (a smoky, heady tuberose scent), Saffron Amber (a blend of amber, ylang ylang and jasmine) and Vetiver Oud (a mix of tuberose, Haitian vetiver and myrrh) are

key scents, all from 2011. Illuminum also makes the Aromarizor, a black box that when plugged in emits fragrance into the air. A team of perfumers, including Rhydian Gwynn Jones, works with the company, which in 2012 opened a perfume lounge on Dover Street, London.

Escentric Molecules

Developed by Geza Schoen, a perfumer based in Germany, the fragrances Molecule 01 (2005), Molecule 02 (2008) and Molecule 03 (2010) are designed to react with each wearer's pheromones to create a unique scent. These perfumes focus on one individual note, rather than the more traditional composition of base note, top note and heart note. They are mainly composed of ISO Escentric 01, which contains a very high concentration of the synthetic woody ISO E molecule, a molecule that is used to create a particular effect – the effect of allure – rather than contribute a fragrance. It has a subtle velvety, woody note, but you rarely smell this fragrance on yourself; rather its appeal is in the effect it has on others.

James Heeley

James Heeley studied philosophy and aesthetics at King's College London before working with the floral designer Christian Tortu in Paris. His interest in perfume was fired by a chance meeting with Annick Goutal (pp. 29–31), and he launched his own brand in 2006. His unusual scents consist of a unique mix of French and English style. Cardinal (2006) is an ecclesiastical scent, with frankincense, myrrh, vetiver and white linen. Mente Fraiche (2006) is light and sweet, very similar to spearmint with notes of peppermint, bergamot and green tea. Esprit du Tigre (2008) was inspired by the Eastern scents of camphor and spices, and smells of cinnamon, cloves and fresh mint.

Juliette Has a Gun

Juliette Has a Gun, which was created in 2006, takes as its inspiration Juliet Capulet, Shakespeare's tragic heroine. It is the brainchild of Romano Ricci (the great-grandson of Nina Ricci and the young heir to the perfume empire behind the classic fragrance L'Air du Temps, a bottle of which is sold every seven seconds). Ricci launched Juliette Has a Gun at Colette in Paris when he was just twenty-eight. The perfume is seen to be Juliet's weapon, and such anti-perfume names as Calamity J (2009; with wood and amber) and Not a Perfume (2010; a crisp and clean single-note scent) suggest the kind of rebellious characters the brand aims to please. There are seven original scents, and a refillable purse fragrance in the shape of a bullet is available for four of them. Mad Madame (2012) has notes of iris, tuberose and patchouli; Lady Vengeance (2006) and Miss Charming (2006) are light rose fragrances; and Midnight Oud (2009) is a vibrant and opulent oriental perfume. Another edgily titled scent, Citizen Queen (2008), is an original chypre aldehydic fragrance with leathery notes.

Le Labo

Le Labo was started by two friends, Fabrice Penot and Eddie Roschi, who met while working in Giorgio Armani's fragrance laboratory. Keen to do something different, they started Le Labo in 2006 with ten fragrances made by well-known perfumers. Le Labo has an edgy aesthetic; it blends the essential oils with alcohol and water when you buy the perfume, and provides customized labels for the bottles. Each perfume is tailored to the city in which it is sold, so the fragrances available to buy in New York differ from those in the London shop. The company now has six boutiques, and its perfumes can be bought in department stores throughout the world.

Nasomatto

Alessandro Gualtieri has built up one of the most unusual niche brands in Nasomatto (literally 'crazy nose' in Italian), which he started in Amsterdam in 2007. Born in Milan, Gualtieri trained in Germany at fragrance company Haarmann & Reimer before moving to Amsterdam. He had previously composed scents for Versace, Helmut Lang, Romeo Gigli, Fendi and Diesel. Black Afgano (2009), one of his most renowned scents, emulates the smell of hashish. There are hints of drugs and alcohol in the names of his other perfumes, among them Duro, Absinth, Hindu Grass, Narcotic Venus and Silver Musk (all 2007), China White (2008) and Pardon (2011). Gualtieri has imposed a limit on the number of products that can be bought online by the same person, to prevent the fragrances from being sold on and thereby to ensure exclusivity. Unusually, Gualtieri does not reveal the ingredients of his perfumes, describing them rather as feelings or quests.

Ruth Mastenbrœk

Ruth Mastenbrœk has worked as a perfumer for more than twenty-five years. One of her finest works was the iconic grapefruit candle she created for Jo Malone (pp. 97–99). It was adored by many celebrities, including Jennifer Lopez, who bought more than 100 at a time and is said to have requested them in every hotel at which she stayed. In 2010 Mastenbrœk launched her own fragrance line. Her signature scent, Amorosa (2012), a combination of tuberose and watermelon, was inspired by her love affair with Italy and serves as a reminder of her quest to make her home there.

Six Scents

This New York-based perfume company was started in 2007 by Kaya Sorhaindo and Joseph Quartana as a side project. Today, their perfumes are stocked in more than 200 stores worldwide. The company pairs six star perfumers, including Stephen Nilsen (the man behind Madonna's Truth or Dare scent, 2012), Mark Buxton and Rodrigo Flores-Roux, with six fashion designers who may not yet have reached the stage at which they can produce their own fragrance, and gives them the opportunity to express themselves through scent. There have been collaborations with Richard Nicoll, Gareth Pugh, Preen and the Brazilian designer Alexandre Herchcovitch.

Tauer Perfumes

Andy Tauer taught himself to make perfume after reading Mandy Aftel's *Essence and Alchemy: A Book of Perfume* (2001). In 2005, at the age of thirty-seven, he left his job as a sales and marketing executive for a pharmaceutical company in Switzerland and founded Tauer Perfumes, an independent perfume house. His perfumes, including the highly regarded L'Air du Désert Marocain (2005), are now sold throughout the world. Completely self-taught, Tauer creates all his fragrances by himself. His unique pentagon-shaped bottles are made by Waltersperger, one of the finest glass-makers in the world.

Union

The British perfume house Union was launched in July 2012 by a group of four businessmen from each part of the British Isles. They came up with the idea for the company as they wanted to create a range of perfumes that would remind them of their youth. The resulting collection celebrates fragrances from each corner of the British Isles, and consists of four fragrances: Holy Thistle; Quince, Mint & Moss; Celtic Fire; and Gothic Bluebell. They were all created by Anastasia Brozler, a bespoke perfumer who composes all kinds of scents (even the smell of a sports-car exhaust for one of her more demanding clients). All the ingredients are specially sourced from the United Kingdom.

Glossary

absolute A concentrated, fragrant oily mixture extracted from the concrete using solvents rather than distillation. Produces fresher, more faithful aromas than essential oils (which are produced through distillation).

accord A balanced blend of several raw materials that unite to produce one new, harmonious scent.

aldehyde An organic chemical that is also present in nature, including in roses, made up of carbon, hydrogen and an oxygen atom. Aldehydes have been used in perfumery since the late nineteenth century.

ambergris A strong, woody-smelling substance secreted by the sperm whale. Ambergris was traditionally used as a fixative in perfume, but – owing to its rarity and price – is now usually replaced by synthetic compounds.

anosmia The inability to smell. This can be a temporary or permanent affliction owing to inflammation or blockage, or the destruction of one temporal lobe of the brain.

base note The third and last note of the perfume (after the top note and the heart note), responsible for giving the underlying tones of the fragrance and for its lasting quality on the skin.

bigarade Bitter orange, also known as Seville orange. Its zest is used to make the bigarade note in perfume.

champaca A flowering tree of the magnolia family, originally found in India, also called the 'joy perfume tree'. Also traditionally used in Indian incense.

chypre French for 'Cyprus'. First used by François Coty to describe the aroma he found on the Greek island, and given to the perfume he launched in 1917.

civet Civet musk is produced by a gland of the Ethiopian civet cat. When diluted, civet adds depth and musky scent to fragrance; it also acts as a fixative. Most modern fragrances now use synthetic substitutes.

clary sage A herb of the salvia family that has an earthy, fruity and floral aroma with a nutty, herbaceous edge. The essential oil is described as smelling sweet to bittersweet, with echoes of amber, hay and tobacco.

concrete A fragrant waxy substance produced from a plant material as a result of extraction and distillation.

coumarin A compound with a sweet fragrance, usually derived from the tonka bean but also found in lavender, sweetgrass and other plants. In high concentrations, coumarin produces notes of tobacco and aldehydes, making it a valuable ingredient for masculine perfumes.

distillation The process whereby scented molecules are evaporated by steam to produce a distillate.

drydown The final phase, or bottom note, of a fragrance, which emerges several hours after application. Perfumers evaluate the base notes and the tenacity of the fragrance during this stage. After the top notes have faded, the heart (or middle) and base notes mingle, forming the body of the scent, the drydown or end notes, which linger on the skin.

enfleurage The process of extracting the aromatic essences from plants using odourless fats to absorb the natural oils. The fat is then dissolved in alcohol to separate it from the essence, and the product is distilled to remove the alcohol. First used by the Egyptians, this method was developed in Grasse in the eighteenth century.

expression The extraction of essential oils from citrus fruits by rupturing the small cells containing the oils.

extraction The process of removing raw materials from plant and animal substances by using solvents. It was developed in the nineteenth century to extract the properties of such raw materials as rose, jasmine and orange.

extrait The highest concentrated form of perfume, a solution of 15–30% perfume oil in high-grade alcohol.

flacon A perfume bottle, from the French for 'flask'.

fougère From the French for 'fern', a name given to a category of perfumes. A fougère accord is created by combining oakmoss, lavender and coumarin.

frangipani The common name for Plumeria, a tropical flower. Frangipani is also known as West Indian jasmine.

frankincense A gum resin from a tree found in the Middle East and Africa. It is harvested by making an incision in the bark; the sap leaks out and is left to harden before it is collected. Frankincense is extensively used in many Christian churches.

headspace technology An analytical technique used mainly to capture the aroma released by plants, flowers, fruit, etc. The substances are captured in an absorbent filter, analysed and identified in a laboratory, then reconstructed. This has allowed perfumers to replicate the notes of flowers, plants and food substances that do not otherwise allow themselves to be used for extraction.

heart note The second note of the perfume (after the top note and before the base note), forming the main body of the scent and serving to mask the base notes until they have mellowed. Also known as the middle note.

heliotrope The flowers of plants from the genus *Heliotropium*, which have a sweet vanilla-like fragrance with undertones of almond.

hesperidia A general term for citrus oils.

indole A chemical compound that smells floral at low concentrations and fecal at high concentrations. Used widely in perfumery, it is also found naturally in some floral notes, such as jasmine, tuberose and orange blossom. The term 'indolic' usually means that a fragrance has a decidedly overripe or animalic characteristic.

infusion The use of oil and unheated alcohol to make tinctures from flowers and plants, so that they can be used in perfume.

ISO E Super An aroma chemical that is used to impart fullness and subtle strength to fragrances.

jasmine A fragrant white, yellow or red subtropical flower, intrinsic to many perfumes.

ladanum An aromatic gum that originates from the rock rose. The sweet, woody scent is similar to ambergris, and can also be used to impart a leather note.

maceration The process that renders a perfume olfactively stable. Maceration is the result of various physio-chemical reactions between the perfume components and ethyl alcohol, and is one of the last stages in the preparation of perfume. The concentrate is left to rest in 96% proof alcohol for several weeks or months to strengthen.

melograno Italian for 'pomegranate'.

neroli An oil from the blossoms of either the sweet or the bitter orange tree. True neroli is created using steam distillation, whereas 'orange blossom' is usually extracted with solvents.

nose (French: *nez*) A person who mixes fragrance components to make perfume; another term is perfumer, or, in French, *parfumeur createur*.

note An aspect of a perfume's range. The top note, for example, is the first impression a person has of a fragrance.

oceanic A synthetically produced fragrance that evokes qualities of the ocean, such as kelp and sea air.

osmanthus A flowering tree from China, valued for its delicate apricot aroma.

oud or oudh Arabic for 'wood'. In perfumery this usually refers to agarwood, found in certain evergreen trees from Asia. Long favoured in the Middle East, its smoky, woody scent has become increasingly popular in Western scents.

patchouli A bushy shrub originally from Malaysia and India. Patchouli has a musty–sweet, spicy aroma.

perfume organ A traditional fan-shaped wooden unit reminiscent of a musical organ, in which raw materials are arranged to give the perfumer easy access.

pomander A perforated ball filled with aromatic ingredients, including spices, woods, and dried herbs and flowers.

pomelo A citrus tree from South-east Asia, with fruit similar to grapefruit.

Rose de Mai Rose absolute made from a hybrid of *Rosa centifolia* and *R. gallica*.

sandalwood One of the oldest known perfumery ingredients; the powdered wood is also used to make incense. Indian sandalwood is now endangered, so many modern perfumes use Australian sandalwood or synthetic substitutes.

sillage The trail of scent left behind by a perfume. Fragrances with minimal sillage are often said to 'stay close to the skin'.

soliflore A fragrance that focuses on or re-creates the aroma of a single flower.

tonka bean A thumb-sized pod from a plant native to Brazil, which smells of vanilla with strong hints of cinnamon, cloves and almonds. It is cheaper than vanilla pods, and sometimes used as a vanilla substitute.

top note The first impression given by a perfume, immediately after the bottle is opened.

vanilla An ingredient taken from the seed pod of the vanilla orchid, a flowering vine native to Mexico (although most of the vanilla available today comes from Madagascar). The flower itself is scentless. True vanilla requires extensive hand-processing and is therefore expensive.

vetiver A grass with heavy, fibrous roots from which can be distilled an oil with the scent of moist earth with woody undertones.

ylang ylang The Malayan name for *Cananga odorata*, an Asian evergreen tree. It means 'flower of flowers'.

Further Reading

Mandy Aftel, *Essence and Alchemy: A Book of Perfume*, New York (North Point Press) 2001

Benedetta Alphandery, *Iris: Il profumo dei fiori*, Milan (Idea Books) 1998

Françoise Aveline, *Chanel Perfume*, transl. Sandra Petch, New York (Assouline) 2003

Elisabeth Barille and Catherine Laroze, *The Book of Perfume*, Paris (Flammarion) 1995

Chandler Burr, *The Emperor of Scent: A Story of Perfume, Obsession and the Last Mystery of the Senses*, London (Heinemann) 2003

Roja Dove, *The Essence of Perfume*, London (Black Dog) 2008

Jean-Claude Ellena, *The Diary of a Nose: A Year in the Life of a Parfumeur*, London (Particular) 2012

——, *Perfume: The Alchemy of Scent*, New York (Arcade) 2012

Elisabeth de Feydeau, *Diptyque*, Paris (Perrin) 2008

——, *L'Herbier parfumé: Histoires humaines des plantes à parfum*, Toulouse (Editions Plume de Carotte) 2010

——, *A Scented Palace: The Secret History of Marie Antoinette's Perfumer*, transl. Jane Lizop, London (I.B. Tauris) 2006

Frédéric Malle, *On Perfume Making*, Berlin (Angelika Books) 2012

Edwin T. Morris, *Scents of Time: Perfume from Ancient Egypt to the 21st Century*, New York (The Metropolitan Museum of Art) 1999

Edmond Roudnitska, *Une Vie au Service du Parfum (A Life in the Service of Perfume)*, Paris (Thérèse Vian) 1991

Luca Turin, *The Secret of Scent: Adventures in Perfume and the Science of Smell*, London (Faber and Faber) 2006

—— and Tania Sanchez, *Perfumes: The Guide*, New York (Viking) 2008

Museums and Collections

Europe

Andorra

Museu del Perfum
Fundació Júlia Bonet
Av. Carlemany, 115, 1er. Pis al Centre Júlia
Escaldes-Engordany
museudelperfum.net

France

Galerie-Musée Baccarat
Place des Etats-Unis
75116 Paris
baccarat.fr/fr/univers-baccarat/musees/
gallery-opening-hours.htm

Galimard Factory and Museum
73, route de Cannes
06131 Grasse
galimard.com/index.php/en/
visit-to-grasse.html

International Perfumery Museum
2, boulevard du Jeu de Ballon
01630 Grasse
museesdegrasse.com

Molinard Factory and Museum
60, boulevard Victor Hugo
06130 Grasse
molinard.com/en/visite.html

Musée des Arômes et du Parfum
de Graveson-en-Provence
Ancien chemin d'Arles
13690 Graveson-en-Provence
museedesaromes.com

Musée Baccarat
rue des Cristalleries
54120 Baccarat
baccarat.fr/fr/univers-baccarat/musees/
museum-opening-hours.htm

Musée du Flacon à Parfum
(Perfume Bottle Museum)
33, rue du Temple
17000 La Rochelle

Musée Parfumerie Cyrnarom
29, avenue Emile Sari
20200 Bastia
Corsica

Museum of Perfume
9, rue Scribe
75009 Paris
fragonard.com/parfums_grasse/
GB/fragonard/paris

Museum of Perfume
20, boulevard Fragonard
06130 Grasse
fragonard.com/parfums_grasse/GB/fragonard/
grasse/the_museum_of_perfumes.cfm

Osmothèque
36, rue du Parc de Clagny
78000 Versailles
osmotheque.fr

Perfume Promenade
Château de Chamerolles
45170 Chilleurs-aux-Bois

Théâtre-Musée des Capucines
39, boulevard des Capucines
75002 Paris
fragonard.com/parfums_grasse/GB/fragonard/
paris/le_theatre_musee_des_capucines_et_sa_
boutique.cfm

Germany

Fragrance Museum Farina-Haus
Obenmarspforten 21
50667 Cologne
farina.eu

Italy

Borsari Collection
Perfume Museum
via Trento, 30/A
43100 Parma

Spain

Museu del Perfum
Fundació Planas Giralt
Passeig de Gràcia, 39
08007 Barcelona
museudelperfum.com

Americas

United States

Annette Green Perfume Collection
Fashion Institute of Design and Merchandising
919 South Grand Avenue
Los Angeles, CA 90015
fidm.edu

Centre of Olfactory Art
Museum of Arts and Design
2 Columbus Circle
New York, NY 10019
madmuseum.org

Cuba

Perfume Museum
Calle Oficios
Old Havana
oldhavanaweb.com/museums/
perfume_museum.html

Asia

Japan

Izu Lake Ippeki Museum of Perfume
843-8 Yoshida
Ito City
414-0051 Shizuoka Prefecture

Museum of Fragrance
2019-15 Tateno
Iwata City
438-0821 Shizuoka Prefecture

Oita Fragrance Museum
48-1 Kita-Ishigaki
Beppu
874-0915 Oita Prefecture
oita-kaori.jp (in Japanese only)

Picture credits

Index

Bold page numbers indicate main references; *italic* numbers refer to the illustrations

Acqua della Regina 9
Adelaide d'Orléans, Princess 93
Aftel, Mandy 181
L'Air du Temps 94, 178
Albert, Prince Consort 87
Alexander I, Tsar 113
Alexandra, Queen 145
Almairac, Michel 40
Alphandery, Eugenio 163–64
ambergris 15
Amouage 13, **19–23**
Antonia's Flowers 14, **33–37**
Arden, Elizabeth 121
Armani, Giorgio 179
L'Artisan Parfumeur 14, **39–43**, 146
Arts et Parfums 83
Ashley, Laura 146
Asprey of London 19
Avedon, Richard 169
Avicenna *8*, 9

Baccarat *53*, *54*, *85*, *88*, *90*, *91*, *93*, 158–59, *158*
Bailey, David 29
Balmain, Pierre 12, 151
Beauchamp, Karen 131
Beaux, Ernest 11
Bellanca, Antonia 33–36
Beni, Fra Damiano 163

bergamot 15
Bersch, Ivan 146
Bienaimé, Robert 94
Billot, Marcel 94
Birkin, Jane *130*, 131
Blahnik, Manolo 67
Blood Concept **175**
Boadi, Michael 177
Bodenham, Edward 73, 77
Bodenham, John 73
Bodenham, Michael *76*
Bond No. 9 **175**
Borghese, Princess Pauline 113, *115*
Boucheron 94
Bourdon, Pierre *80–81*
Bourjois 12
Brooke, Amelia Eliza *85*
Brooke, Simon and Amanda 14, *85–91*
Broudoux, Roger 118
Brozler, Anastasia 181
Bucelli, Friar Cosimo M. *164*
Burr, Chandler 17
Bury, Brigitte 158–59
al Busaidi, Sayyid Hamad bin Hamoud 19
al Busaidi, Sayyid Khalid bin Hamad 19
Buxton, Mark 180
By Kilian **176**
Byredo **176**

Calèche 13, 19
Calle, Sophie 121
Cambridge, Duke and Duchess of, *see* William,

Prince of Wales and Catherine Middleton
Cameron, Samantha 127
Carles, Jean 12, 128, **131**
Caron 12, *158*, 183
Carthusia 15, **45–51**
Cartier 13
Carven 128, 131
Casino Royale 166
Castelli, Giovanni 175
castoreum 15
Catherine de' Medici, Queen of France 9, 163, 164–66
Cellier, Germaine 12, 151, 153, 155
Chanel 127, 131, 171
Chanel, Gabrielle (Coco) 7, 11
Chanel No. 5 11, 12, 15, *17*, 94, 127
Chant, Bernard 34
Charles of the Ritz 127
Charles-Roux, Edmonde 169
Châtillon, Jean-Hugues de *122*, 125
Chaumet 79
Chevalier, Georges 158–59
Chong, Christopher 19, *19*, 20–23
Christian, Clive 14, **53–57**
Christian, Victoria 53, *53*, 57, *57*
Churchill, Winston 59, 73, *74*, 146
citrus expression 16

civet 15
Clinique 34
Conte-Sévigné, Fabienne 43
Coty 157
Coty, François 11–12, *13*
Coueslant, Yves 67, *67*
coumarin 11
Craig, Daniel 166
Craven, James 62–65
Creed 10, **59–65**
Creed, Erwin 59, 60, 65
Creed, James Henry 59, *59*
Creed, Olivia 65
Creed, Olivier 59, 60–62
Cresp, Oliver 148
Crickmore, David 20
Crown Perfumer 14

Dana 131
Delveaux, Thérèse 83
Deneuve, Catherine 67
Diesel 179
Dietrich, Marlene 101, 151, 155
Dior, Christian 12–13, 19, 79, 83, 131, 151, 169
Diorissimo 12–13, 83
Diptyque 43, **67–71**
distillation 16
Donati, Enrico 94–95
Dove, Roja 7, 9, 57, 86, 95, **157–61**
Doyen, Isabelle 29, 30–31
Duchaufour, Bertrand 39, *39*, 40, 146–48
Dupont, Bertrand 82

Eau d'Hadrien 13, *28*, *29–30*, 31
L'Eau de la Reine 163
Editions de Parfums **80–83**
Egypt, ancient 7–8, *7*
Elisabeth, Empress of Austria 59
Elizabeth II, Queen 146, 159
Ellena, Jean-Claude 7, 39, *78–80*, 82
enfleurage 15–16, *16*
Epinette, Jerome 176
Escentric Molecules **177**
Eugénie, Empress 59

Fargeon, Jean-Louis 9, 113, 122
Fashion Fragrances and Cosmetics 151–52, 153
Fendi 107, 179
Ferrero, Lucien 118, *118*, *119*
Feydeau, Elisabeth de 9, 122
FiFi (Fragrance Foundation) 27, 57, 161, 183
Fitzgerald, F. Scott 101
Flanders, Angela 15, **25–27**
Fléchier, Edouard *81*
Flipo, Anne 40
Florence 9, 15, 166
Florentin, René de 9
Flores-Roux, Rodrigo 95, 180

Floris 10, **73–77**
Floris, Juan Famenias 10, 73, *73*
Fontaine, Thomas 118
Fougère Royale 11, 95, *95*
Foyle, Shelagh 73, 74–77, *76*
Fracas 12, 94, 151, 152–53, **155**
Fragonard 10, *16*
Fragrance Foundation 27, 57, 161, 183
frankincense 7, *11*
Franz Joseph I, Emperor of Austria 59, *61*

Galimard 10
Galliano, John 71
Gallimard 82
Garces, Joe 152
Gardner, Ava 60
Gaultier, Jean Paul 121
Gautrot, Christiane 67, *67*
George III, King 59
George IV, King 113
George V, King 59, *86*, 88
Giacobetti, Olivia 39–40, *43*, 70, *81*, 118, *118*, 176
Giboulet, Henri *115*
Gigli, Romeo 179
Giorgio Beverly Hills 12, 13
Givaudan 95, 131, 133, 152
Givenchy, Hubert de 82, 151
Gorham, Ben 176

Gossip Girl 166
Goutal, Annick 13, **29–31**, 43, 178
Goutal, Camille 29, 30–31
Grasse 10, *10*, 57
Grindley, Polly 73
Grojsman, Sophia 79, 82, 133
Grossmith 14, 57, **85–91**
Grossmith, John 85
Gualtieri, Alessandro 179
Gucci 152
Guerlain 11, *15*, 43, 157, 161
Guerlain, Jacques 133
Guerlain, Pierre 133
Guichard, Aurelien 12, 152–53
Gwynn Jones, Rhydian 177

Haarmann & Reimer 179
Halston 34
Hammer, George 158
Harris, Lyn 10, **127–31**
Haute Parfumerie, Harrods 158, *158*, 159
headspace technology 16
Heeley, James **178**
Hempel, Anouska 139
Hennessy, Kilian 176
Henry II, King of France 164
Hepburn, Audrey 102, 124–25
Herchcovitch, Alexandre 180
Hermès 7, 13, 19, 39, 43, 79, 83
L'Heure Bleue 11
Hopkins, Anthony 166
Houbigant 9, 10, 11, **93–95**
Houbigant, Jean-François 93
Hungary Water 15
Hy, Michael 13

Illuminum **177**
iris root 15
Iskia 43
Islam 9

jasmine 10, *10*, 15
Jenner, Christopher 70
Jesus Christ 7
Jicky 11, 161
Jo Loves 97, **99**
Jo Malone London **97–99**
Joan, Queen of Anjou 45
Josephine, Empress 93, 113, *115*, 118
Juliette Has a Gun **178**

Kelly, Grace 60, 101, 115, *117*
Kennedy, John F. 59–60, 102
Kenzo 94, 152
Kerléo, Jean 136
Klein, Calvin 13, 82, 94
Knox-Leet, Desmond 67–70, *67*
Krigler **101–105**
Krigler, Albert 101–102, *101*
Krigler, Ben 102–105, *102*
Krigler, Kri Kri 102
Krigler, Lea 102
Kurkdjian, Francis 9, 12, **121–25**

Le Labo **179**
Laboccetta, Mario 45, 50
Lacroix, Christian 79
Lagerfeld, Karl 67
Lalique, René 12, 93
Lancôme 133
Lang, Helmut 179
Lanvin, Jeanne 11, 121
Laporte, Jean-François 39, 43
Latoui, Mohamed 71
Lauder, Estée 12, *12*, 33, 82, 97, 98–99, 127
Lauren, Ralph 82
Lautier Florasynth 133
lavender *10*, 15

Lelong, Lucien 11
lemon 15
Lempereur, Olivier 83
Louis-Philippe I, King of France 113
Lubin 10, 43, **113–19**, 158–59, *159*
Lubin, Pierre-François 113
Lutens, Serge **169–73**
LVMH 157

Maack, Andrea 17, **174**
Mabel, Emily 148
Madonna 29, 107, 151, 155, 180
Maison Francis Kurkdjian **121–25**
Malle, Frédéric 13, 14, 43, **79–83**
Malone, Jo 14, **97–99**, 180
Maria Amalia, Queen of France 113
Marie Antoinette, Queen of France 9, *9*, 93, *112*, 113, 118, 122
Marlborough, Duke of 145
Marsh, Christopher 73
Mary, Queen 86, 88
Mastenbroek, Ruth **180**
Mauriac, François 82
Melchio, Richard 128
Michau, Jean-Louis 134
Middleton, Catherine 54–57, *54*, 77, 88, 177
Miller Harris 10, 14, **127–31**
Mitsouko 11, 15, *15*
Mitterand, François 70
Molinard 10
monasteries 15
Monroe, Marilyn 73, *74*, 151
Montand, Yves 43
Moses 7
Moulton, Nicola 131
Mugler, Thierry 148
Mülhens 115
musk 15

Nagel, Christine 99
Napoléon III, Emperor 59, *61*
Napoléon Bonaparte, Emperor 93, 113
Nasomatto **179**
Nicolaï **133**, **37**
Nicolas II, Tsar 59
Nicoll, Richard 180
Nilson, Stephen 180

Obama, Michelle 127
orange blossom 15
Ormonde Jayne 14, **139–43**
Osmothèque, Versailles 136

Pagani, Michele 45, 48
Paquin, Jeanne 11
Parquet, Paul 11, 93–94
patchouli 27
Patou, Jean 94, 127, 136
Penhaligon, Leonard 146
Penhaligon, Walter 145, 146
Penhaligon, William Henry 145, 148
Penhaligon's 40, 43, **145–49**
Penn, Irving 169
Penot, Fabrice 179, *179*
Perrault, Micheline 29
Perris, Elisabetta 93, 95
Perris, Gianluca 95
Perris, Michele 95
Pescheux, Olivier 71
Pfizer 12
Pickles, Sheila 145, 146, *146*
Pickthall, Michael 146
Piguet, Lucien 98
Piguet, Robert 12, 94, **151–55**
Pilkington, Linda **139–43**
Piver, L.T. 11
Poiret, Paul 11, 151
Polges, Jacques 131
pomanders *8*
Preen 180

Prés, Honoré des 43
Prot, André 114
Prot, Paul 114
Prot family 113
Proust, Marcel 14, 82
Pugh, Gareth 180
Putman, Andrée 83

Quartana, Joseph 180

Rahmé, Laurice 175
Rawyler, Fred 122, 125
Ribeiro, Júlio 163
Ricci, Nina 94, 151, 152, 178
Ricci, Romano 178
Rivière, Caroline 9
Rizzie, Dan 36
Robert, Guy 13, 19
Robertet 29, 43, 86, 128, 133
Rochas 19, 83, 133
Romans 8–9, *8*
Ropion, Dominique 79, *79–81*, 82
Roschi, Eddie 179, *179*
Rose de Mai 10, 53, **57**
rose water 9
Rosenthal, Joel Arthur (JAR) 13
Rotherham, Sarah 148
Roucel, Maurice 80, 81, 82, 171
Roudnitska, Edmond 12–13, 82, **83**
Roudnitska, Michel 79–81, 82
Rubinstein, Helena 136
Ruocco, Silvio 48

Saint Laurent, Yves 13
Santa Maria Novella 9, 10, 14, *14*, 15, **163–67**
Schiaparelli, Elsa 131
Schlienger, Monique 128, 131
Schoen, Geza 177
Schving, Paul 94
Schwieger, Ralf *81*
Scolari, Francisco 34
Shakespeare, William 178

Sheldrake, Christopher 171–73
Shiseido 43, 169
Sieuzak, Lucas 19, 23
Sisley perfumes 39
Six Scents **180**
Smart, Ellen 146
Sorhaindo, Kaya 180
Squillace, Giuseppe 110
Stefani, Cesare Augusto 163
Sting 107
Süskind, Patrick 15–16, 79

Taittinger Group 30, 31
Tauer Perfumes **181**
Theophrastus 110
Thevenin, Gilles 115–18
Tonatto, Laura 48
Tortu, Christian 178
Trumper's 146
tuberose *10*, 15

Union **181**

Van Cleef & Arpels 13, 127
Venice 9
Versace 179
Victoria, Queen 14, 54, 59, 60, 85, *87*, 93
Villoresi, Lorenzo 12, **107–11**
Vinchon, Karine 40–43
Vionnet, Madeleine 11
Vogue 169
volatile solvent extraction 16

Waltersperger 31, 181
Warhol, Andy 11
William, Prince of Wales 54–57, *54*, 77, 88, 177
Wulff, Pierre 176

Yourcenar, Marguerite 29

Zuddas, Antonio 175

Acknowledgements

I dedicate this book to my daughter, Ocean, who gives me eternal motivation and whose beautiful spirit is a constant source of joy.

My most grateful thanks to the team at Merrell: Claire Chandler, for her heartfelt encouragement and never-ending enthusiasm for the project; Rosie Lewis, for her inspiration and delicacy; Nicola Bailey, for her artistic and visionary designs; Nick Wheldon, for his determination and unsurpassed professionalism; Annie Jordan for her kind and helpful support; and Hugh Merrell for his interest in the book.

A huge thank you also to the stars of the show, the perfumers and perfume houses, for their unfailing help and encouragement. Special thanks to Gianluca Foà for his indomitable enthusiasm and kindness. Also my deepest gratitude to many long-time friends who have helped me, and to those who have become new friends during the course of my work on the book.

Listed right are just a few of those who have helped to make this dream become reality. And, of course, my indebted thanks to my partner and my family, who have always helped in countless ways.

Paris Ahmadpour
Benedetta Alphandery
Helen Arthur
Anila Baig
Bane
Colin Barr
Antonia Bellanca
Joanna Berryman
Candida Bond
Jack Cassidy
Gloria Castellazzi
James Craven
Steve Curtis
Pascale Daninos
Nanci Derienzo
Susan and Kiva Fateh
Joe Garces
Rebecca Gentry
Azzi Glasser
Camille Goutal
Polly Gredley
Jane Harper
Joanne Harris
Mona Hlali
Alexia Inge
Anita Kaushal
Millie Kendall
Fiona Kennedy
Elizabeth Lyon
Dora and Fiona McBride

Charlotte McCarthy
Jenna McLooey
Trish McFadden
Sonia Scott McKay
Louise McKenna
Adil Magik
Meg Mathews
Opinder Mehmi
Ann Miller
Larissa and Ade Opanuga
Linda Pilkington
Richard Reyes
Michelle Roques-O'Neil
Natasha Sakota
Kerry Smith
Laury Smith
Allan Stewart
Deborah Thomas
Megan Toland
Mai-Vi
Giles Vickers-Jones
Sandrine Wagner
Jason Waterworth
Daisy Waugh
Alek Wek
Ann Williams
Bill Williams
Maggie Williams

First published in 2013 by Merrell Publishers, London and New York

Merrell Publishers Limited
81 Southwark Street
London SE1 0HX

merrellpublishers.com

Text copyright © 2013 Tessa Williams
Illustrations copyright © 2013 the copyright holders; see p. 188
Design and layout copyright © 2013 Merrell Publishers Limited

British Library Cataloguing in Publication Data:
A catalogue record for this book is available from the British Library.

ISBN 978-1-8589-4577-4

Produced by Merrell Publishers Limited
Designed by Nicola Bailey
Art Assistant: Tom Lobo Brennan
Project-managed by Rosanna Lewis
Indexed by Hilary Bird

Printed and bound in China

All quotations from featured perfumers are taken from interviews with the author, unless otherwise stated.

Page 183: Fragrances by Nasomatto (see p. 179)
Page 184: Classic fragrances by Grossmith (see pp. 85–91)
Page 187: A monastery flower-garden; see Carthusia (pp. 45–51)
Page 188: Muguet de Luxe perfume bottle; see Lubin (pp. 113–19)
Page 192: Iunx by Olivia Giacobetti (see p. 43)